ALSO BY ISOLINA RICCI

Mom's House, Dad's House

EPL - MILNER

Mom's House, Dad's House for Kids

Feeling at Home in One Home or Two

ISOLINA RICCI, PhD

A FIRESIDE BOOK

PUBLISHED BY SIMON & SCHUSTER

New York   London   Toronto   Sydney

FIRESIDE
Rockefeller Center
1230 Avenue of the Americas
New York, NY 10020

Copyright © 2006 by Isolina Ricci, PhD
All rights reserved,
including the right of reproduction
in whole or in part in any form.

FIRESIDE and colophon are registered trademarks
of Simon & Schuster, Inc.

For information regarding special discounts for bulk purchases,
please contact Simon & Schuster Special Sales at 1-800-456-6798
or business@simonandschuster.com.

Designed by Jan Pisciotta

Manufactured in the United States of America

10   9   8   7   6   5   4   3   2   1

Library of Congress Cataloging-in-Publication Data is available.

ISBN-13: 978-0-7432-7712-9
ISBN-10:   0-7432-7712-0

This book is dedicated to you, the reader.

Contents

PART III BELIEVE IN YOURSELF

PART IV EXTRAS

Mom's House, Dad's House for Kids

Meet Dr. Isa

Hi, I'm Isolina Ricci. Kids call me either Dr. Isa (EE-sah) or just Isa. For many years, I have been a counselor, teacher, and mediator for lots of families where the parents were separated, divorced, or remarried. I also taught other counselors, teachers, lawyers, and judges about what families need. Many parents and grandparents know who I am because I wrote the book for adults called *Mom's House, Dad's House.*

Kids and their parents have taught me a lot about what is important to them. My own kids (I have five of them) also went through my divorce. Now my kids are all grown up and doing well with families of their own. I'm a very happy grandmother (six of my grandchildren are between the ages of ten and fourteen). For fun, I love watching my grandkids play soccer or baseball, dance, do karate, or ride horses. I always enjoy hearing about their projects, playing games with them (they usually win), cooking or drawing together, telling stories, and watching major league baseball together.

A Message for Parents

Mom's House, Dad's House for Kids is an inside view of separation, divorce, and forming a stepfamily. It is primarily for children ten and older to read alone or with their parents. It is meant to be an encouraging and realistic friend that empowers children with practical ways to gain understanding, some perspective, and self-knowledge. It's an operating manual with a message: Believe in yourself, take pride in your family, and use times of change to get stronger and learn important life skills. Many children will be relieved to read this book because it can affirm and express their experiences. If you also read this book, your child can take comfort in knowing that you have the same frame of reference—especially with delicate subjects like anger, panic, and feeling disloyal or in the middle.

As a parent, you know the challenges you face as you divorce or remarry. These family changes can bewilder and upset children even when you assure them that things will turn out well down the road. But, take heart; children can and do travel successfully through major life transitions, especially when they know parents love them and are doing their best to steer the course. You have this book because you sincerely want to do the right thing for your child. You may have already covered many of the topics in this book with your child (or are well on your way). If so, this book can help your child remember your advice, validate your perspective, and continue being open with you. If you and your children are just beginning the process of transition, then this book can be useful in offering ideas, concepts, and guides for your consideration. If you have younger children between the ages of eight and ten, they can also benefit from this book if you select passages and read them together. If your child is younger than eight, you can read the book yourself for ways to help your child express feelings. Children between six and eight may seem self-sufficient, but they can be much more vulnerable to fears and misunderstandings. Select topics cautiously, rephrase them in your own words, and encourage questions.

The three goals for this book are to

1. Offer the reader maps through divorce and stepfamily territories with defined regions, things to know and do, a sense of what's ahead, and the final destination.

2. Establish a sense of order and structure around major transitions with enough information to empower but not overwhelm.

3. Reinforce your role as a parent by encouraging your child to strengthen certain life skills and attitudes that foster resiliency. These skills can help children bounce back from tough times and also believe in themselves and in their future.

Your child will probably enjoy this book best when read a few pages at a time. Encourage him or her to take it slowly. If your child is shy about expressing a feeling or a desire, you might suggest that he or she point to a page or leave a marker on pages for you to read. Please do not pressure your child to read certain passages. Children have their own internal wisdom that tells them when they are ready to deal with their feelings and when to share them with others, including their parents. Some children will not verbalize their feelings, but are more comfortable expressing themselves by drawing, writing in a private journal, engaging in fantasy play or games, or through physical activity. You know what's "normal" for your child. If you feel uneasy about his or her behavior, do discuss your concerns with a trained counselor or your pediatrician.

Finally, and this might be the last thing you want to hear right now, healing and adjustment always seem to take more time than we expect. During big transitions, children require more, not less, attention from parents. But, this often comes at a time when parents are preoccupied with heavy responsibilities and major life transitions. So, treasure those little ways where you reassure your child that you will always love and take care of them—no matter what. You are your child's safe haven.

FUTURE
BELIEVE IN YOURSELF
DREAMS
GOALS
STEPFAMILY
SINGLE PARENT FAMILY
DIVORCE
SEPARATION

Kids—Read This Page First

This book is about how to stay strong, feel better, and succeed in life when your parents separate, divorce, or get married again. It has tips, exercises, and examples that encourage you to develop skills for "bouncing back" from puzzling or difficult situations and ways to get smarter and stronger. Learning these skills can help you your whole life.

You can't do anything about your parents' big decisions—especially about separation, divorce, or getting remarried. But, you can do a lot to help yourself. This doesn't mean that everything will always feel great or that you won't get discouraged. But, it does mean that step by step you can feel stronger and more confident. You can find ways that work for you. Even when things take more time than you want, you can still get there. This book shows you how.

No matter what happens with your parents now, you will eventually grow up to have your own separate life as a young adult. This book will encourage you to believe in yourself and follow your dreams. You can do a lot more than survive. You can grow up to become the successful person you are meant to be.

What's Happening to You Now?

Maybe your parents are just talking about separation or divorce, or it happened a while ago. Maybe one or both of your parents remarried, or it's just happening now. No matter if you live in one home or two, you will find some ideas, answers, and problem solvers that could work for you. No book can deal with every family situation, but you should be able to find some things here that will be useful for your life now and later on.

How to Read This Book

Read this book a few pages at a time. You don't have to start at the beginning. Go to the pages that are most interesting first. Other pages will be more interesting later. Each chapter has information for different situations with lots of stories, lists, and examples.

 The pages in this book are like the pieces of a big puzzle. So, if you want the whole picture, you eventually have to read it all.

Here are some of the things you'll find in this book:

 Tips are ideas you can try anytime—today, next week, or whenever.

 Words to Try are suggestions you can think about when you want to speak up.

Train Your Brain exercises are ways to learn important skills like getting organized, solving problems, or succeeding.

Let's get started!

Part I

Separation and Divorce Territory

SEPARATION AND DIVORCE TERRITORY

Separation and divorce are a little like a long road trip. The destination is a new version of normal family life—one that is different from what you knew before but is still right for your family.

Your family's road trip might be short and simple, or it might be long and complicated. Things may seem better for a while, then worse, then much better. The road might be fairly straight, or curve back and forth. Every family's trip is different. But no matter what happens along the way, try to remember that you can use what you learn to help you stay strong and get smarter about things. Eventually things will settle down and you will arrive at your destination. There may be moments when it feels as if your world is coming to an end, but it won't. However, it *is* changing.

SNEAK PREVIEW OF SEPARATION AND DIVORCE TERRITORY

1. **Splitting and Dividing.** This is just before and after your parents' separation. For some families, it's shock and

weirdness time. You may hear your parents arguing. You wonder what's true and what's not. You'll find out about your feelings, how to feel better fast, and how to use a "special energy." You will also find out how to stay out of the miserable middle of your parents' problems and get some straight answers to your questions.

2. **Changes and More Changes.** This is when your parents have started living in two different places. Some kids have just a few changes. For other kids, there are a *ton* of changes to get used to. This is why this chapter is so long. Whether you are in one home or two now, you will find out about living in a new home, new rules, and new routines. You will find ways to stay connected with your parents, family, and friends; deal with stuff at school; see grandparents and other relatives; and celebrate holidays. You'll probably still have some strong feelings about everything while the adults are figuring it out. With good information and ideas, things can be much easier.

3. **New Ways.** Here is where daily life gets much better even though people may still have a bad moment or even a bad day. By this time, you and your family have settled into routines and schedules. Feelings have settled down, too. You'll find tips in this section on how to handle yourself when your parents are meeting new people, different ways to solve problems, and how to work together as a family team. Even though you may have some surprise "creep-ups" of old feelings, life is a lot more fun as you reach your destination—a new kind of normal family life.

Your parents' separation and divorce is one of the biggest things that will ever happen to you. So, no matter if the divorce was years ago or if it's happening now, you can decide to help yourself understand better, gain important life skills, and go on to succeed in life.

Remind Yourself

- I can help myself in lots of different ways.

- I can use my experiences to get stronger and smarter.

- I can figure out how to handle things as my family changes.

Chapter 1

Splitting and Dividing

The time before and just after the parents split up can be painful. Kids can feel suddenly different. Their feelings might be hurt a lot. Maybe they feel shocked, sad, or scared. Even when parents say everything will eventually turn out okay, some kids can feel as if they are in the middle of an earthquake or bad dream.

"This is the WORST day of my LIFE!" Daria shouted to her parents. "I don't WANT you to divorce! I want things to stay THE WAY THEY ARE NOW! How could you do this to me!" Daria's little brother started to cry. Later, she listened as her parents explained how they would take care of them as they always had, only now it would be in two homes instead of one. That helped, but Daria still felt awful.

The twins Zoe and Amy knew their parents had problems. Mom and Dad were grouchy with one another, and their father had been sleeping in the den for a long time. When their parents said they had something important to talk about, Zoe whispered to Amy, "Divorce."

That was last week. While Amy felt as if her world was falling apart, Zoe wasn't upset. She was just going to see what happened.

When Luke's mom told him last month that his dad wasn't coming back home, Luke felt relieved. He won't have to worry about Dad being drunk and acting crazy. His mom said things will work out much better for everyone. Luke still felt weird and wondered if his father still loved him.

Ben slammed the door to his room. He didn't want to listen to his parents' ugly fighting again. Dad had moved out two months ago, but that didn't stop the arguments. Now Mom said she was going to get full custody, whatever that meant. No one ever told him anything, and his sisters were no help. He put on his headphones and turned the volume way up.

Justin's father said, "It's been four months since your mom and I separated. How are you doing with all this?" Justin smiled and said, "Things are okay, don't worry." But things were not fine. He and his older brother did not let their parents know how they felt. Justin was very sad, and when he was alone he cried a lot. He also thought he was to blame for the split. He just couldn't talk about these things.

Do any parts of these stories sound familiar? It can be hard for kids to explain what they feel. One thing, for sure, kids have a *lot* of big questions.

SOME BIG QUESTIONS

Why are things so weird? What's going to happen?
When will I see Mom or Dad? Why can't they just fix it?
Where will I live? Is my family ruined forever?
What do I do with my feelings? Who can I believe?
Is this all my fault? Will we move away?
Will I still see my friends or
change schools?

WHAT'S TRUE ABOUT DIVORCE

- **Your parents still love you very much.** They always will.

- **You can't get your parents back together.** You can tell them how you feel, but you can't make them do anything.

- **The divorce is definitely *not* your fault.** What's happened is totally your parents' responsibility.

- **You can try to get answers** to your most important questions. Your parent is your first choice of a person to talk to. If you don't think that will work, find a trusted adult to talk to.

- **The hardest changes usually work out eventually.** But it takes time.

- **There are important things you can do to become stronger and smarter,** and there are ways to help your parents.

- **You still have a real family.** Even if your family feels "broken," it's not. Instead, it has divided into two parts. Some things are different from before, but it is still your family, and it is real. You can be proud of it.

- **Some things often get much better after the separation.** That might seem impossible to believe, but later this can be true. Your parents will usually be happier. That's good for you, too.

- **It's the parents' job** to take care of their kids. Parents will figure out arrangements for school, transportation, activities, and lessons, and who will be there for you. So try not to worry about adult responsibilities.

WHAT'S NOT TRUE

- I feel the separation is my fault. **NOT TRUE.**

- My parents have problems because of me. **NOT TRUE.**

- I can get my parents to change their mind and get them back together. **NOT TRUE.**

- I am not worth anything. I am not important to anyone. No one really cares. **NOT TRUE.**

- Nothing I do makes any difference, anyway. I might as well do anything I want, even if I get into trouble, or just play video games all day. **NOT TRUE.**

- I need to know everything about the divorce. I want to know why this is happening and who is to blame. **NOT TRUE.**

These not true thoughts can make you miserable and ruin your day. They can upset your relationship with a parent or your siblings. These thoughts can be difficult to get rid of by yourself. Talk to an adult you can trust, such as a parent, a close relative or friend, your doctor, or a counselor. Just remember that these negative thoughts are NOT TRUE.

YOUR FEELINGS

Everyone has lots of feelings when parents split, especially at first. You—and your parents, too—can feel shocked but at the same time be afraid, sad, or mad. All these feelings can also be mixed in with special feelings called grief. Grief is more than just being sad. It's the deep feelings and thoughts that come when you no longer have someone or something in your life that you loved very much.

At first, you can feel you have lost something precious. It can feel like there is a big hole in your life that you don't know how to fill. Not having both your parents together anymore is one of the biggest things that will ever happen to you (or your parents), so grieving is natural. Both adults *and* kids will need time to adjust to the changes and to their new way of living and being a family. It doesn't happen all at once. And sometimes it feels like a very long trip. But eventually things will get a lot better.

Most of the time feelings are mixed together—just like a soup. And they can be intense at first. You can love your parents, but at the same time you can also be mad at them for getting a divorce. All these feelings can be mixed in with feelings of grief. Not only that, but you can feel one way today and another way tomorrow. If any of this is happening to you, you are not weird. It's a normal first reaction to big changes. All people have their own type of "feeling soup," even though they may not show it.

If you feel like this, you are not weird or different.

It's a normal first reaction to big changes.

These feelings don't last forever. There are things

you can do to help yourself feel better.

Some kids are very upset at first. Then they start figuring out what the changes mean. Others take longer to digest what's happening. One girl is ready to ask her mother questions. A boy her same age doesn't want to talk to his parents about *anything* yet. He still feels too sad. Some kids blame a parent for the separation or for having to move or change schools. They might even pick a fight. They might be rude or mean, or get into serious trouble when they didn't do things like that before. But there are other kids who aren't too worried. They may decide like Zoe just to wait and see what happens.

If what's happening is scary instead of cool,

your feeling soup can taste awful.

HOW TO FEEL BETTER FAST
BY YOURSELF

- **Breathe slowly and deeply about three times.** Then go back to your regular breathing. This will give your brain the oxygen it needs so you can think better and choose what to do. If this doesn't work right away, wait a few minutes and then breathe slowly and deeply again three times.

- **Tell yourself, "Calm down, stay cool."**

- **Tell yourself, "I'm not weird, it's just my feeling soup. Things will get better. Millions of other kids have survived times like this. I can, too."** You could write these words on a piece of paper and keep it in your pocket or backpack. This is a way to "train your brain" to overpower feelings.

- **Take charge by taking a run or doing something that takes a lot of energy.** One of the fastest ways to feel better is to do something that makes your body move. The next section, "Use Your Special Energy," explains this.

- **Do something else.** Change the subject of your thoughts. Try reading, playing electronic games or sports, playing an instrument, listening to music, or hanging out with friends. Do whatever works for now.

- **Make a "feel good" list.** Your list might say something like, "petting my cat, reading, playing soccer, being at a friend's house, talking to Grandma." Keep this feel good list close by and do one or two of these things to feel better.

- **Draw or write.** Draw a picture of your feelings or your thoughts anytime you want. Or write poetry or keep a private journal. It's good to express your feelings and thoughts. It helps get things out. You can keep these private or share them.

- **Hang out with your feelings.** Go ahead and feel sad, mad, hurt, or just upset. Your feelings will settle down after a while, especially as you learn how to take charge of them and get clearer about what you want to have happen in your life. It's okay to feel mad, but it's not okay to hurt yourself or someone else or something because you are mad. It's not okay to do something that will get you in to trouble.

- **Think back.** Do you remember how you felt when something scary or bad happened in the past? What did you do that made you feel better? Did things get better for a while? You can ask parents or friends what they have done.

- **Spend some time by yourself.** Maybe being alone is more comforting. Big changes often require time for your brain and body to take it all in. You can do some of the things on this list when you are by yourself.

- **Learn how to make your energy work for you.** This is explained in "Use Your Special Energy" on the next page.

WITH OTHER PEOPLE

- **Talk it out** with an adult you trust. If a parent is reading this book with you, you might explain what's in your own feeling soup or maybe write it in a note or letter. If you can't talk to a parent right now, talk to a good friend. Ask what they have done. If you feel bad a lot, talk to your parent about seeing a counselor for a while. Good talking almost always helps.

- **Give and get extra hugs.** Hug your parents, grandparents, siblings. Ask for hugs back. Spend time with people you feel close to.

- **Talk with friends on the phone, spend time with friends or family doing fun things.** Talk about your interests, things at school, or activities, or do fun things with others where you don't think about the divorce. If you are on the Internet, try instant messaging.

- **Hang out with your pet.** You can cuddle or talk to a pet or stuffed animal. When you take care of a pet by taking it for walks or runs, grooming its coat, or feeding it, you can feel useful. Your pet will appreciate it, too.

Use Your Special Energy

What is "special energy"? When big changes bring up shocked or scared feelings, our mind often send signals to our body saying, "Get moving, give me more power and energy! Be careful!

Something big is happening here!" This is special energy. Some people just call it adrenaline. It happens when the survival part of our brain thinks we are in danger.

How Special Energy Works

Our earliest ancestors had to outsmart and sometimes destroy predators such as saber-toothed tigers in order to survive. To do this, their bodies gave them a supercharged dose of hormones (including adrenaline and cortisol). This gave them a special kind of extra energy either to stay and fight for their lives, run away, or freeze or hide (so the predator wouldn't see them). These hormones sent more blood and oxygen to their muscles and organs, making them much stronger. After the special energy calmed down, their bodies needed extra rest to recover from the big effort.

But there was one problem. Their brains didn't get as much oxygen. It was mostly going to their muscles and organs. Our bodies still work like this today. This is why it's important for you to stop and breathe deeply several times whenever you feel your special energy surging. Good breathing will send more oxygen to your brain so you can think clearly and use that special energy at the same time!

We all can have this special energy rush in whenever we are frightened, shocked, super-emotional, stressed, or super-excited. The survival part of our brain thinks we are in real danger, so the special energy switch in our body gets turned on to high, higher, or highest. Big changes like separation, divorce, or a new stepfamily can feel scary, so they bring up this energy, too. Although your parents might tell you things will work out with the divorce, your ancient survival instinct isn't so sure. So even though your life is not really in danger, your special energy switch can get turned on.

When Daria's parents told her about the divorce, her brain said, "Big changes!" and her body went on "high alert." Her heart started to beat faster, and she started yelling and fighting with her parents. For days afterward, Daria felt all wound up tight and not like her old self.

When Justin first heard the news, he felt frozen inside. He just wanted to stay in his room, listen to his music, or be online. His grades went down because he couldn't concentrate in class. He wondered if he was turning into someone weird, but he couldn't seem to help it.

Ben had a different reaction. During the first months after the separation, he had lots of feelings. But during the most intense times, he just wanted to run and run. He felt like there was an engine inside that was roaring to move or it would blow up.

Amy didn't know what to do. Sometimes when she thought about the divorce, her voice, knees, or hands shook or her arms feet prickly, or she had butterflies in her stomach. Sometimes, she felt like throwing up or was panicky.

Sometimes kids like Daria or Ben feel their special energy wanting to get out. At other times, it might stay inside and get swirled with their sadness and grief over losing their old life, like it does with Justin and Amy. Maybe you are able to pick out the times right now when your special energy is flowing in your body. When your body is growing fast, you might not be able to identify special energy easily. But be patient. In time, you will be able to feel when this special energy is in your body, so why not use it to help you—or learn about it for the future?

Many people have learned how to use special energy to help them excel or focus. Sports team talk about playing with intensity. Kids talk about being "up" to a challenge. Top athletes have learned how to make sure their brain gets enough oxygen in order to think clearly but also keep plenty of extra energy in their muscles so they can perform at their best.

What to Do with Special Energy ⭐ TYB
The next time you realize that you are feeling that intense energy, here's what to do.

1. First thing, BREATHE (this is the same breathing as described in the "How to Feel Better Fast" list on page 14). Breathe in and out slowly two or three times—*no more or you might get dizzy*. Then breathe normally. These breaths give your brain the oxygen it needs so you can think better and choose what to do next.

> **TIP** *If it's too hard to breathe slowly, try this. Breathe in, counting in your mind "1-2-3," hold your breath counting "1-2," then breathe out as slowly as you can. The slow breath out is what relaxes you. Repeat this once or twice, then breathe normally.*

2. TELL YOURSELF, "STAY COOL, CALM DOWN."

3. TELL YOURSELF: Say to yourself, **"What I'm feeling is probably my special energy. It's a normal reaction. Eventually, I'll learn how to use this energy to help me get stronger and smarter."** Try not to skip this step. Remember, you're training your brain to pay attention to your energy.

4. THINK! Where can you use your extra energy right now? Take a run? Practice something? Clean your room? Do something that might otherwise be hard to do. Your energy may make it easier this time.

> **TIP** One time you may be able to use this energy for homework or projects that need quiet and concentration. Other times your body wants to move instead of concentrate. Just go with it.

5. LEARN ABOUT YOURSELF. When that special energy rushed in on you, what did you want to do—fight, flee, or freeze?
   - Was I like Daria? Was I furious and fighting with words or my fists? Was I just being stubborn or mean? Did I feel especially courageous?
   - Was I like Ben, wanting to run away? Did I want to pretend that what was scaring me was not really happening?
   - Was I like Justin, feeling frozen, going in slow motion with my special energy trapped inside?

- Was I like all of them at different times or something different from all of them?

6. Later, when you are feeling more like your relaxed self again, plan where you would like to use this extra energy in the future to get smarter and stronger. Maybe you will use it to practice a sport, or concentrate more on a school subject or something you want to get really good at. The older you get, the better you will become at training your brain to know when special energy comes up. You can say to yourself, "Hey! It's special energy. I can probably use it the way I want."

> Special energy can help you get braver,
>
> better, smarter, and stronger.

Daria realized that she usually felt good during and after she was at soccer, so she started practicing more. She actually seemed to see better, run faster, and be a better player. She started to feel a lot stronger. She even started studying more with some friends. She fought less with her parents, too. She couldn't do anything about the divorce. But she could be in charge of her life at school and with soccer. Besides, when she was busy, she didn't think about all the changes or feel so sad about her parents' split.

Luke felt sad and a little mad that his dad couldn't be like other kids' dads. At the same time, he also felt a lot of tension and frustration. It was as if some of the crazy energy was left over from the way things used to be when his dad was at home. He got in trouble at school because he was losing his cool over little things. His baseball coach assigned extra batting practices and conditioning. The extra exercise made Luke, just like Daria, feel a lot better. He and his coach set some goals for his performance. Luke now felt more confident and clear about his goals. He was staying cool.

When Justin started taking his dog out for a run every day, he started to feel better. He slowly came out of his freeze mode. Although he took more interest in school, he still didn't want to talk about things. Justin was grieving for his old life and missed his mom, especially at night when he was trying to go to sleep. He also felt lonely. He didn't feel there was anyone to talk to. Justin may adjust to the separation and divorce slowly and carefully. This could be the right speed for him.

TIP

If you are like Justin, remember that you need to get moving after a few weeks, so that you can come out of freeze mode. You will still feel your sadness coming and going, but freezing can drag your body and feelings down. Everyone's body needs movement and good food to stay healthy. Also, do your best to get answers to some of your questions. Use your quiet alone times to go over your "feel good" list (page 14), read

Chapter 8, "Take Care of Your Body" (pages 181–187), and see Part III of this book, "Believe in Yourself" (pages 175–226).

When you start paying attention to how you react, you will be learning the language of your own body. Growing up and living your own life is full of all kinds of challenges and decisions. If you can learn how to use your special energy over these next few years, you'll have a *big* advantage for your future

TIP *Playing sports, running, exercising, and other physical activities (like swimming or cutting the grass) often naturally bring more oxygen to the brain. These things also help work off the extra hormones in the body. That's one of the reasons why it's good to exercise regularly when you are under stress.*

YOUR PARENTS AND SIBLINGS

Your Parents Aren't Quite Themselves Either

Your parents, grandparents, and even some other relatives have their own soup of feelings and worries during a big family change such as separation or divorce. They may act differently. Some parents show how sad they are. Some parents may have less patience and be grouchy or preoccupied with other things. They might not listen or pay attention to you as much.

Some parents might say and do things they didn't say and do before. Their children may not know what or whom to believe. Kids can feel scared and sad. If any of this happens to you, try to remember that this is a hard time for your parents, too. Sometimes their feelings spill over. They can't help it. You can leave the room, or you can give them a hug. But however they act, it is not your fault or your responsibility to fix it, so don't try. The next chapter talks more about these things in the section on "Parents."

Who Is Telling the Truth

What if you overhear a parent talking about the reason for getting a divorce. Later, you overhear the other parent saying something different. What should you believe? Is one parent lying? It can be confusing.

Adult relationships can be very mysterious—even to the adults. It's not a kid's job (or right) to know exactly why parents separate or divorce. It's still the adults' private business, and they make the decisions even when these decisions change your life. Sometimes adults explain their side to kids; most of the time they don't. This may not seem fair, but it's been that way forever.

TIPS UNDERSTANDING PARENTS

- Both parents usually believe that their point of view is the correct one. Most parents don't lie about these things.

- Your parents' differences are about adult matters. These are usually not things you need to know or be involved with. Just try to accept the fact that your parents see and feel things differently from each other.

- Your parents' differences led them to separate. These differences show up in how they understand things. As time goes by, they usually accept their differences more. This doesn't mean they'll get back together. But by living apart, it's easier for them eventually to understand each other.

- Your parents may be the most upset, worried, or moody during the time just before and after the split, especially when they are making legal decisions about what changes in your family life and what doesn't. When one parent gets married again, that can also be a hard time for the other parent.

> If your parent won't answer your questions or gets
> upset if you ask, just let it go.

WHOM CAN YOU TALK TO?

Maybe you can talk to or ask your parents about anything that is important to you. But maybe you don't feel you can because they're having a hard time now. Maybe you don't want to. Maybe you told an adult something once that was really important, but the adult didn't believe you or just got mad at you. That makes it hard to trust again. It's not easy to know whom to trust.

Try to Be Open with Your Parents

When you have something on your mind, always consider talking to your parent or grandparent first. Parents usually want their children to talk with them and are often surprised to learn that some of their children are uncomfortable telling them things. But still try to be open with your parents. Maybe you think that your grandparent or another adult would be a better listener of some things. No book can tell you for sure that the person you pick to talk to is a good choice, but here are some suggestions.

TIPS WHO TO PICK

- **<u>Do</u> pick an adult who will not get upset** with you and who will not tell on you. If you can't talk to a parent or grandparent, then think about talking with someone whose job it is to take care of kids or families, such as your minister, preacher, priest, or rabbi. Maybe a parent of a good friend would listen, or maybe there are counselors at school you think you can trust. Librarians can help with some questions.

- **<u>Don't</u> pick a person who gives you an icky or uncomfortable feeling.** That's your internal warning signal saying, "Don't talk to this person about private things."

- **<u>Do</u> pick someone you have known for a while,** at least a year. He or she should be kind, a good listener, and a person you trust. You feel really safe when you are with this person.

- **<u>Do</u> pick a therapist or counselor** if you have a choice. It's their job to make you feel safe, to treat you well, and to keep every single thing you say private.

- **<u>Don't</u> get discouraged if you don't find this special adult right away.** Sometimes parents are too stressed to really listen to you. If that's true for you now, things will probably get better in a while and you can share your thoughts and feelings with them later. Sometimes it's hard to find an adult who is a good listener and who respects what kids have to say and how they feel. Just keep your eyes open and choose carefully.

ARE YOU AN ONLY CHILD?

Some "onlies" feel grateful that they are the only kid in the family. They don't have to compete with a brother or sister for their parents' attention. Nothing gets borrowed or broken by a sibling, and there are no fights between kids. But other "onlies" long for a sibling to share stuff with and to talk to or at least share some of the constant parent attention. It can be lonely if you don't have many friends your own age, especially when parents are so preoccupied with the divorce that you don't feel you are as important as before.

But the opposite can also happen. Your parents can bury you in questions about how you feel, or give you books to read or classes to go to. In their desire to be good parents, they might be constantly (and intensely) observing you so they can evaluate how well you are reacting to the divorce. When this happens, some kids want to say, "Please stop. I'm doing okay. I know the divorce is not my fault. You're stressing me out with all your worries and constant questions."

TIPS FOR ONLIES

- Remember that siblings don't have perfect lives, either. Often, they don't talk to each other about what's happening. They fight, too. It's easy to think that others have it better, when actually what they have is just different.

- Are there other kids your own age you can talk with about what you are going through? What about other relatives or the parents of friends?

- If your parents overanalyze how you feel, maybe you can tell them what you want instead. *"I know you want the best for me, but I would really appreciate it if you would stop asking me so many questions. I know I can ask you what I want to know."* Or you can write your feelings down in a letter and give a copy to each of them.

UNDERSTANDING WHAT YOUR SIBLINGS ARE GOING THROUGH

Having Brothers and Sisters Can Help

If you have brothers or sisters, you might be able to help each other during these changes. Do you think you can all stick together at least some of the time? Okay, so you've heard this before, but life is a lot easier when you have a sibling who is a buddy rather than an enemy. All kids can feel helpless to change what's happening. But you aren't helpless in how you treat one another. You can share what you know, especially if things feel weird around the house.

Separation and divorce affect different kids in different ways. It depends on how old they are. Unless siblings are close to your age, they may act differently from you when they are worried, confused, or full of feeling soup. So be cool. Don't make fun of them or tease them for it. Don't expect them to feel the same way you do. It may only make them feel more alone and confused, especially if they are younger than you.

HOW SEPARATION CAN AFFECT KIDS OF DIFFERENT AGES AT FIRST

- **Babies** can't explain their feelings or understand why things happen. They're just not old enough. Babies feel something inside when their parents or siblings are mad, mean, sad, scared, or rushed. It can feel scary to them. They might cry, whine, want to be held, or be cranky. They might not sleep or eat as well. They feel best when their schedule for sleeping, eating, or being with their family members stays the same. When they don't see you or a parent as much as they used to, they also might act differently. Babies feel safe if they are held by someone they trust. If you pay attention to babies, especially if you bring happy feelings and nice hugs, both of you may feel better.

- **Kids in preschool** may start acting like they did last year or the year before. They may go back to their security blankets, sucking their thumbs, or wetting the bed. They may tell big stories and even think they did something that caused the divorce. Little kids need hugs, understanding, and big brothers and sisters who can make them feel safe. It may be hard to do when your siblings are extra crabby or whiny. But try to remember that they can't express what it is they feel, and they are scared. You are older. You can tell them that things will turn out okay and they will believe you. You probably have to tell them this many times. Be patient.

- **Kids in kindergarten to third or fourth grade** can be especially sad about the separation and cry a lot. They may think up stories about your parents that will scare them. They can feel responsible for your parents. Maybe they act hyper or disorganized. You are still older than they are. They will look up to you, and you can give them a hug and tell them that you will always be together. You can tell them that they don't have to choose a side for either Mom or Dad and that everyone in the family will feel better after a while. You can admit that you have feelings, too, but that you know things will turn out okay after a while. Tell them that they will always have their mom and dad, even though it's in different homes. Do something to make them laugh so they don't think about their worries. Be kind.

- **Siblings ten to fourteen years old** are kids around your age. This book explains a lot of things for you. If you have a sibling or two close to your age, you can help each other feel better because each of you can really understand how the other feels. Try talking about what's happening and sharing what you know. If you have questions or other things you want to talk to your parents about, think about doing it together instead of alone. Try to be partners, and have fun together, too.

- **Older teenagers** have their own brand of thoughts and feelings. They might not want to talk about them to anyone in the family. Teens may act tough, but they're hurting inside, too. You might just hang out together. At least try not to bug them. Don't get too upset when they are crabby. You might ask for their help with what you're going through. This can help you both. Older siblings can feel like they are doing something helpful, and you can use the advice and support. Everything works better when you help each other out.

Got sibling power?

Doing Things Together

Even if in your family the kids are very different ages, it still might feel good to do more things together as brothers and sisters. Are there games you can play? TV shows or DVDs you can watch together? You could help one another with homework or school projects. If you're feeling really generous, you can help each other with chores. The truth is, when kids find ways to stick together, they do better with big changes.

QUESTIONS AND ANSWERS ABOUT SEPARATION AND DIVORCE

Kids usually have lots of questions but are sometimes unwilling to ask them. If you are one of those kids, here are the answers to some of the questions you might like to ask.

My parents say they don't love each other anymore. Can they stop loving me, too?

No way! Adults can divorce each other, but parents do not divorce their children or stop loving them. Adults can stop loving each other in that special way that lets them live together. But it isn't the same between a parent and child. You can ask your parents yourself. Your parents still love you and always will no matter what problems they have. That's just the way nearly all parents are made. Even those parents who are absent for a while (or even a long time) rarely stop caring about their children. But these parents don't act like good parents. Sometimes they are clueless.

Why can't I get my parents back together?

Because this is an adult situation, and it is up to them. You might want them together again with all your heart. You can tell them you want them back together, but you can't make them do it. Pretending to be sick, getting in to trouble, dropping your grades, fighting a lot, hurting yourself, or acting mean will not convince them to change their mind. Doing these things will only make you feel worse and get you in to bigger trouble. Some kids hope that if they are extra nice their parents will go back together. Kids might do things the first time they are asked, do extra-credit work at school, practice longer, or help more with brothers and sisters. Even though these are all good things, they still won't get your parents back together. It may not seem fair, but only adults can decide whether or not they will live together. Think of it this way. If you don't want to be friends with someone anymore, it's not your parents' job to get you back together with that friend.

I feel a little guilty. Does this mean the divorce is somehow my fault?

No way. Separation or divorce is always an adult decision. It's not because of something a child did or didn't do. Sometimes a kid has been angry or upset or has big problems at school. No matter what has happened or what you have done, you are still *not* responsible for what an adult or a parent decides to do or not do. Adults are always responsible for how they act and what they say. If anyone tells you that you caused the split, this person is wrong.

Why did this happen to my family?

You are not alone. About one million kids a year have parents who separate or divorce. Almost all parents have tried their best to stay together. They do not want to hurt their children or each other. But adults need a certain kind of love to be able to live together. This adult love is different from the love parents have for their children. When that kind of love changes, it is often impossible for adults to live together, even though they may still care about each other. When parents realize that things will not get better with time or with counseling, many of them choose either to live apart or to get a divorce. Parents are usually sorry when this has to happen.

Do most kids know the divorce is coming?

Every family is different. For example, some parents keep their problems away from their kids. They may talk to a counselor, a pastor, or a priest, but they don't talk to their kids. They keep acting as if everything is okay. So the kids have no idea until one day, wham, the bad news comes like a lightning bolt out of the sky. Some other parents fight a lot around their kids, so these kids have a hint that something is wrong. And some kids actually wish their parents would separate because of the fighting. Sometimes even parents don't know a divorce is coming. One parent thinks everything is fine, and then the other announces that he or she is moving out.

Will this divorce hurt my chances to be liked or happy?

No. But remember, every person has to earn his or her own chances for happiness and success whether or not their parents live together. You can do it! What if your legs were seriously harmed in an accident? Wouldn't you want to work with the physical therapist to make your legs work again? Most kids would say yes, even if they felt discouraged or in pain. But if you never worked at getting better, you probably would have trouble walking again. With divorce, even though your parents' problems are not your fault, you will face some challenges and new situations. You can try and get stronger by meeting these challenges instead of thinking that nothing will help. Reading this book will help you decide what to do and how to use these times that you are going through to your advantage.

I think one of my parents is to blame for the divorce. I'm really mad! What do I do?

Talk about this with the parent you think is to blame. You may be worried that your parent will get upset or sad. But find a way to talk about these extra-strong feelings. Buried or stifled feelings can cause more pain and anger. And you may be wrong about why the divorce is happening. Admit to that parent that you need support in figuring out why you feel this way. You might say, *"Dad [or Mom], I know that you are doing what you think is best, but I need your help. Maybe the divorce is nobody's fault, but it's hard to understand."*

I don't think about the divorce much at all, and most of the time I am happy and busy with school and friends. Should I feel guilty. Am I wrong?

No! It's normal to want to feel okay and happy. The divorce belongs to your parents, along with their thoughts and feelings about it. You have your own separate thoughts and feelings. There is no need for you to feel guilty, no matter what your feelings are about it. The divorce is between your parents. It is not your problem. It is important that you keep up with your own activities and feel happy.

THE MISERABLE MIDDLE

Sometimes kids feel like they are in the middle of adult arguments or problems. Some parents might fight in front of the kids, talk badly about each other, or ask kids to carry messages, lie, or act as a spy. Kids can even put themselves in the middle. They can butt in by trying to fix an argument, taking sides, or listening around corners to conversations. No matter how it happens, "in the middle" is a miserable place to be.

How does it happen? Adults can get caught up in their own strong feelings and stress, especially when they are splitting and dividing and when there are changes and more changes. Adults might not even notice what they are doing. They may not understand that what they say or do put a child in the middle of an adult situation. Parents can forget that kids are watching and listening. They may not mean to do it, but it happens anyway. It's not a kid's fault when these things happen.

If your parents are fighting or saying hurtful things, it's not your job to fix it. If you try, you are butting in. And you can't make them change anyway. You may want to be loyal to a parent, but you also need to be loyal to yourself. You are not to blame for your parents' ways of treating one another. And it's not your job to stop them from what they are doing. What you need to do is be loyal to yourself. You deserve respect.

The Tug-of-War Inside You

If your parents put you in the middle, it can make you feel sick inside, sad, scared, mad, or responsible for what is happening.

It can even feel like there is a tug-of-war going on inside you. One part of you is against the other.

Sometimes parents forget that you have both of them inside you. When they do or say bad things about each other, they are asking you not to like a part of yourself. Even if a parent is a real dork sometimes, you don't want to be forced to hear about it or to pretend to hate one of your parents.

Remember, even though you have both parents inside you, they are just one part of you. Your whole person is special and different from your parents.

Some "Miserable Middles" and Words to Try

What if your dad asks you if your mom has a boyfriend. You feel trapped. You want to please your dad, but you know that it's not right to tell him about Mom's private life. If you do tell your dad, you'll feel guilty. Words to try: *"Dad, I really love you, but I don't want to talk about what happens over at Mom's."* (Try)

What if your mom tells you that your father is irresponsible and selfish. Well, maybe he isn't perfect (who is?). Still, it's not right for an adult (your mom) to complain to a kid (you) about another adult. Grown-ups should handle their own problems. Words to try: *"Mom, I trust you. But I love Dad, too, and I want to decide these things for myself."* (Try)

What if your dad doesn't actually say anything bad about your mom, but he gets a scowl on his face when you talk about having fun with Mom. You wonder if your dad is jealous and wants you to love him best or not enjoy your time with your mom. You can give your dad a hug and tell him that it's good to be with him now. You might also decide you won't tell him about your fun with Mom for a while. Sometimes there is nothing you can say for the time being that will change his attitude. Probably he'll feel better about many things after a few months and you can share things with him again.

What if your grandmother and aunt tell you that your mom is to blame for the divorce because her job was more important than her family. You love your mom and your grandmother and aunt. But what do they expect you to say? It feels awful. You know that it's not right for anyone to talk badly to you about your mother. Words to try: *"I don't know why you are telling me this, but it hurts my feelings."* (Try)

What if your dad tells you that he won't come to your school open house if your mother is there. You feel that your dad wants you to choose him over your mom. You don't want to deal with any of this. So maybe you think you have to lie to your dad and mom and tell them the open house isn't important (even though it is). A better way is to tell your dad and mom that the open house is very important to you and that you definitely want them to be there. You tell them that you are not going to be the one to decide who comes, but you want both of them to be there with you.

What if your parents give each other nasty looks when one of them comes to pick you up. Sometimes your parents argue at the front door or at the car window as you are getting ready to drive away. Or maybe they don't speak to each other at all. This really makes you feel bad. It feels as if your parents hate each other. Lots and lots of kids have this situation. It takes a while (sometimes a long while), but most parents do eventually stop being angry and treat each other courteously. Meantime, you can't do much about it. But you (or with your siblings) could write a letter to your parents telling them how you feel when these things happen. Don't take sides or be rude in your letter.

(Try) For example, *"Dear Mom and Dad, We kids would like to ask you to use your best manners when you see each other or talk to each other when we are around. It hurts our feelings and makes us feel sad when we see the way you act to each other or when you don't talk to each other at all. Please, can you stop? We love you both very much and we don't want to take sides or get in the middle."*

You will have to decide how you will get your letter to your parents. You should make two copies, one for Mom and one for Dad. You might mail it with a stamp or you might e-mail it (if you are on the Internet). Many parents can be surprised that their kids are so aware of how they act toward one another. They often try to make changes once they understand how it hurts their kids.

What if your mom is pressuring you to tell your dad that you want to go to summer camp instead of spending time with him this summer. You do want to go to summer camp, but you also want those three weeks with your dad. It's frustrating! You wonder why your parents can't figure it out so you can do both. You're in a hard situation. First, look at the different problem-solving exercises on pages 233–44. Think your situation through using one of the exercises. Then try talking to both your parents separately. Make it clear that you want to do both.

THINGS TO DO WHEN YOU'RE IN THE MIDDLE

* Say to yourself, "This is between them. It's not my business or my problem."

- Leave the room. Go somewhere where you don't have to hear or see it.

- Be patient. As your parents settle into their new living arrangements, they will probably relax and see how their behavior affects others.

- If you continue to be in the middle, talk to an adult you trust. Perhaps he or she may be able to help.

- Remember that these things may help you feel better, but they can't make your parents change.

Miserable Middle Questions and Answers

My mom says my dad has some kind of a serious problem and that's why he's not seeing me now. Should she be talking about him like this?

It sounds more like your mom is trying to protect you, not put you in the middle. But you can ask her, "Why are you telling me this?" Your mom may believe that you have a right to know things that will affect you. It doesn't mean that you are responsible for how either your mom or dad feels or behaves. Remember, you can still love your dad and hope he gets better. But it might mean that the time you spend with him is limited until he gets well. That's what your mom may be trying to tell you.

My dad says he will agree to let me attend the private school I want if my mom changes her attitude toward

him. **I want to go to that school, but what do I do about this "attitude" thing?**

This is a tricky, miserable middle! You want to go to that school. Your dad feels so strongly about his problem with your mom that he's using you as a messenger and holding your schooling hostage. He probably doesn't mean to do this to you. Still, whatever their problems are, it is not something you can fix. But you can give both your parents information about the school and hope they realize what they are doing. If you don't think you can talk to them about it, write your own note or letter to each of them explaining why you want to attend. Do you have handouts or materials about this school that explain class size, subjects, and activities? If yes, include these in your letters to your parents. If not, you could call the school and ask them to send the information to you. This proves to both your parents that you are serious about making the change. It might help. If it doesn't, you will know you tried. You know you can't control an adult's behavior.

YOUR RIGHTS AS A KID

- I have the right to refuse to carry messages from one parent to the other.

- I have the right to leave the room when my parents argue. If that's not possible, I have the right to ask them to please not argue in front of me.

- I have the right to love both of my parents equally and not take sides.

- I have the right to not listen to anyone who says mean or disrespectful things about my parents.

- I have the right to refuse to spy on a parent or grandparent or other family member.

- I have the right to refuse to lie to a parent or family member.

- I have the right to not worry about family money problems.

- I have the right to love and honor (and spend time with) each of my parents and all of my relatives, even when they don't get along with each other.

- I have the right to not worry that my parents will take away their love from me or stop seeing me if I don't do everything they say.

- I have the right to be loved no matter what.

When Kids Put Parents in the Miserable Middle

Kids can feel hurt, neglected, or deprived when their parents split. Some kids think about getting revenge for having to go through the family changes of separation or divorce. Other kids want their parents back together so much that they will say and do things just to get their parents to talk to one another. Other kids just want to mess with their parents and watch them fight or act foolish.

Kids can be tempted to get their way by putting their parents in the middle (or making them feel guilty). Do you ever mouth off at your parents about the divorce or say mean things to them about how you don't like your life now? Do you sometimes say things that aren't true? Do any of these things help you get your way? If yes, you know what you are doing and what these things are.

Have you ever done things like these?

- Told one parent the other parent approved of something when that parent didn't approve of it at all. Told your dad, "Mom said okay," but Mom never really did.

- Tried to get your parents to feel guilty about the divorce so you will get more things. "Other kids have credit cards for clothes. Just because you got divorced shouldn't mean I have to suffer."

- Told about things that go on at the other house in order to keep your parent's attention. "Dad's new girlfriend doesn't have any children and she is a lot younger than you."

- Told one parent that the other parent is better or that the other home is nicer. "It's much nicer at Mom's and she lets me watch TV anytime I want."

- Threatened a parent with moving to the other house if you didn't get your way. "They appreciate me. I'm moving there!"

- Told one parent that the other parent did something awful that wasn't true. "Mom left me alone, all night."

- Tried to get one parent to talk to the other parent for you about something you wanted or did. "I just can't talk to Dad. I'm afraid to say anything. Please, please, please talk to him for me."

- Told one parent that the other parent said that he or she missed him (or her) when that parent didn't say any such thing. "Mom, you know that Dad says he misses you."

It's not always easy to go on this separation and divorce journey with your parents. And you have a right to your feelings. But be careful about putting your parents in the middle, or just being sneaky or not telling the truth to get your way. You don't want them to do it to you. Don't do it to them either.

Why Is the Separation/Divorce Journey So Hard Sometimes?

For a while, kids and parents can grieve and miss the way their life used to be. Grieving and feelings are both nature's way of helping us adjust to the loss of one way of living and accepting a new one. Everyone does this in their own way and at their own speed. While this is happening, family life is changing, there is "feeling soup," special energy, and temptations to get stuck in the miserable middle or put someone else in it. It's a *lot*. And sometimes it is hard.

TIP *When you feel sad and miss the way things used to be, try a few things from your "Feel Good" list on page 14.*

The next chapter, "Changes and More Changes," looks at the changes you and your family might go through and things that can help make those changes easier and even fun.

I can choose ideas, tips, and words

that help me grow stronger. I can help myself

build life skills I can use my whole life.

Chapter 2

Changes and More Changes

This part of separation and divorce territory is full of new experiences. Once a parent moves out to another place, family changes usually pick up speed. For some kids, there are just a few changes, but for others there are lots of them—big and small. Do you like change? Some people do, but others would just as soon things never changed, ever. Change is a part of life, divorce or not. Some family members miss the old ways of doing things, and others are relieved with the new ways, especially when the parents stop fighting. It's normal for anyone to still have plenty of feeling soup and lots of questions. Because parents are usually extra busy managing all the household changes and their legal business, kids may feel as if parents aren't listening to them as much as they used to. But, kids need answers.

Don't worry. Your life will feel like your own again, even with all the new things. With time, you will figure out how to feel comfortable with your new way to be a family. Eventually, your parents will settle the legal business and life will be easier.

SOME BIG QUESTIONS

Where am I supposed to be this week?
Who picks me up? Where do I sleep? What about
school and friends? How can I remember? What if I don't
want to go? Will I still go to camp? Will I see my
grandparents and cousins? How can I make
my life feel okay again?

TIP *This is the longest chapter in the book because some kids have many questions and changes to figure out. If you don't have so many, just look through this chapter quickly and pick out the parts best for you.*

The Saddest Part Is I Miss You

The saddest part is missing a parent. You don't have both parents at the same time all the time. And that is a huge difference. "You are always missing a parent at first," said Amy. Maybe you miss playing ball in the yard, the little game you play before you sleep, the talk in the kitchen. Although these times can be really tough, you and your parents can find many ways to stay connected when you are apart. Over time, some kids find that communications with a parent are better than ever and that they have time with a parent in a way they didn't have before.

The Second Saddest Part Is Missing Pets

If you have a pet and live in two homes, you might bring it with you back and forth. Or you might have pets at both homes. What if you have to leave them behind? When you leave, you miss your pet. And when you are gone, your pet misses you. Maybe a parent doesn't have a place for a pet, so you don't have a choice. Cheer up. Your pets will learn that even though you are gone sometimes, you will come back and still love and play with them.

GREAT WAYS TO STAY CONNECTED

Make staying connected super-important. The list below can help, but come up with your own creative ways. If your parents give you a cell phone, you can do many of the things below. If they don't think a cell phone is a good idea, you can still do just about everything listed below if your parent uses a phone or voice mail. Many kids find that staying connected with parents can make the changes easier and fun. Communicating helps you figure things out, make good decisions, and deal with your feelings. See if the things below will work for you now. If not now, come back and try them again in a month or two.

CONNECT THROUGH

- PHONES and VOICE MAIL

- REGULAR MAIL

- PICTURES by mail and e-mail

- NOTES left for a parent to read later

- TAPE-RECORDED MESSAGES

- PRIVATE TIMES TO TALK—like an appointment

- A SPECIAL SPOT—cubby, box, or envelope—where you put things you want your parent to read or have

- SAVING JOKES to share later or mail

- AN ACTIVITY, MUSIC, or SPORT you play or enjoy together

- A PICTURE OF THE OTHER PARENT AT EACH HOME

- A JOURNAL of your thoughts that you may want to share

- A REGULAR "DATE" with a parent every week or two for uninterrupted time alone together

- VIDEO HOOKUPS with a camera where you can see each other when you talk on the phone or computer

- CELL PHONES, TEXT MESSAGING, E-MAIL, IN-STANT MESSAGING—for older kids with permission from their parents

Zoe and Amy didn't see their dad for two months after he moved 1,000 miles away, even though they talked on the phone several times a week. At first, they were both "dad sick," feeling sad and with an ache in their chests. They missed him so much. Dad used to joke with them and help with special school projects. It was better when Dad and Mom got them their own cell phones for their fourteenth birthday. Now they talk every day. They are also sharing some school projects again with Dad, using e-mail. Next month, their mom is getting a video phone hookup so they can actually see their dad and he can see them. They are excited about this.

Daria and her brother call either parent anytime they want. But both of them had to learn to use good judgment. At first, Daria was so upset about things that she was calling her parents many times a day at work about things that could wait until they all were at home. Now Daria has settled down and she calls her parents a few times a day—unless there is a real problem and then she calls anytime. The kids are now trying to find an activity that they can do with their dad, such as hiking or learning how to rock-climb.

Ben doesn't have e-mail or a cell phone, but he and his mom have a place in the kitchen where they leave notes for each other. His mom now works two jobs, one at an office in their home, the other in an office downtown. They use a tape recorder on the kitchen counter and leave messages that way. When his mom is at the downtown office, he always calls her when he gets home from school or from his activities. Ben is angry that his dad doesn't call more often. Ben thinks maybe he will start calling his dad instead of waiting for his dad to call him.

Justin keeps a picture of his mom and dad in his wallet and has one in his room. His mom travels a lot, but he calls her when he comes home from school every day and sometimes again at night. He calls his dad at work whenever he wants, so he feels connected. But, still, he misses being with his parents.

Luke doesn't have any contact with his dad. Sometimes things happen where a kid just can't or should not be in touch with a parent. Luke decided to write his dad some letters that he would never mail. It felt good just to write them. He might want to give these letters to his dad someday when he sees him again. Or he might not. He'll decide then.

ONE HOME, TWO HOMES

Different Families, Different Ways to Live

Families have many different kinds of living arrangements. Kids can have a family in one, two, or even more homes.

Daria and her brother are with their mother one week and with their father the next week. Their dad moved into a house about a mile away. Daria says she has two homes.

Amy and Zoe's father moved far away, so they live with Mom during the school year and with Dad two months during the summer and on certain school breaks. But the twins still feel like they have two homes.

Ben's dad lives temporarily with Ben's grandfather in his small apartment in the next town. Ben and his sisters still live with their mom in their old apartment, and they take turns staying over at their grandfather's about once a month. Ben says he has one home.

Luke has one home. He doesn't see or talk with his dad at all right now. He and his mom live in the same place. Now he goes to his aunt and uncle's house after school, and their place is beginning to feel like a second home.

A family can have more than one or two parents and siblings. Kids can also live with grandparents, other relatives, stepparents, stepsiblings, and close friends. For example, the parents separated and their house was sold. The kids went from having one home to two new homes. One home was with their mom and grandparents, the other with their dad. Eventually Dad remarried and the kids had a stepmother, a great-aunt, and two stepsiblings. In some cases, siblings split up and one lives with Mom most of the time, the other with Dad most of the time. When kids get into their teens, some don't want to move back and forth as often.

Sometimes kids have some things similar to how they were before the split. One family rented the same vacation cabin during the summers and lived in an apartment during the school year. After the divorce, the kids still lived in these same homes with Dad plus a new home with their mom. There are also kids who have three parents in three homes. One with Mom, one with Dad, and one with a stepparent who is no longer married to one of their parents. Many stepparents deeply miss their stepkids and want to stay in their lives after they are no longer married to the parent.

> Just remember, no matter who makes up
> the people in your family, it is just as good as
> anyone else's family.

When parents separate and one of them goes to live in another place, there are lots of things to think about. There may be a new schedule for you and new ways to celebrate holidays or go on vacation. You might move some or all of your stuff into a new place in a new neighborhood. You might have to transition from one home to another often, or maybe not. You still have school and friends to think about. For sure you have to think about how to get along with your parents. You may have to deal with parents who seem to be more distant or not around much. There are grandparents and other relatives to think about, too. It might help if you got some information on what all this legal divorce business is all about.

Calendars and Schedules: Keeping It All Straight

Maybe you have one home now and visit your other parent a few times a month. Maybe you don't see your other parent much or at all. Or maybe you spend a lot of time with both parents and have two homes. Whatever arrangement you have, the following tips on getting organized and traveling can be helpful. After all, kids travel for lots of reasons besides divorce schedules. Maybe you are with a relative or friends overnight. Maybe you have to keep track of different rides with different people after school. Being organized always helps no matter what you are doing.

If you have two homes, you have to be organized. How else can you keep the schedule straight and remember what to bring, what to leave, what to pick up? It's easy to forget school announcements, schoolbooks, homework, or clothes that go back and forth. It can make parents and kids cranky! Look at these tips and try them out. You can become an expert at this.

You need a schedule. It's easy to get upset when you or a parent forgets a party or a test or someone remembers it at the last minute. Or you forget that you're going to be with your other parent that day, or you forget the time you are supposed to be ready. There are different ways to keep the schedule straight. Some kids have a homework planner or calendar in their backpack where they write in the days they are with each parent. Other kids don't write down the schedule because they think they will remember (But very few people have memories that good.) Other kids count on their parents to remind them.

Some parents try to keep a big calendar of everyone's schedule in a place where the whole family can read it (like the refrigerator door). This is called a "master calendar."

Since there are usually changes to put on a calendar like a new doctor appointment or a new practice or test date, even a master calendar can miss stuff. So keeping things straight means either you write things down for yourself or you *really* pay attention to what your parents tell you about today and this week.

No matter what you decide about how you keep your schedule, be sure to get the answers to these FIVE BIG QUESTIONS before you leave the house to be with your other parent. (This works for all other times you go someplace, too.)

THE FIVE BIG QUESTIONS

1. WHERE am I going?

2. WHO takes me and picks me up or how do I get there?

3. WHAT TIME?

4. WHERE DO I GET PICKED UP or take transportation?

5. WHAT STUFF DO I NEED?

Kids and parents try different ways to keep things straight. Todd, whose parents had been separated just a few weeks before, made his own calendar and wrote in the answers to the Five Big Questions. It was a lot of work, but it made him feel

---

Rachel's Answers to the Five Big Questions

WHERE am I going? __With DAD for the weekend__

WHO takes me and picks me up? __DAD picks me up after soccer__

WHEN and WHAT TIME? __Friday—5:30 pm__

PLACE where I get picked up? __small parking lot next to baseball field__

STUFF that I need? __soccer clothes, homework, library book__

---

better. He kept this folded in his pocket and carried it with him. Rachel took a regular calendar she had and asked her mom to help her mark the days she would be with her and with Dad. A different mom and dad have a Central Command Calendar in each of their homes. If there is a change, they tell each other by phone or e-mail and they write it down. You can find your own way to keep things straight that works for you. Don't be afraid to ask your parent for ideas.

YOUR JOBS

1. Take responsibility for getting the answers to the Five Big Questions on those days when you are going to transfer from one home to the other. It can make everybody's life easier and prevent confusion, disappointments, and hurt feelings.

2. Do your part by bringing home school announcements, bulletins, and handouts—and ask for two copies so each

parent gets one. Your parents need you to cooperate so they can help you meet your school requirements.

Be sure to let your parents know right away when you have half days at school, special events, or parties you want to go to. Don't wait to tell your parents! It's too easy to forget, so put it on your own calendar, too.

| TIP | **Remind your parents about your activities.** You know how it feels when you are so busy you forget things. But you also know how it feels when someone forgets something really important to you. It's especially hard when parents don't remember, don't show up when they should, or don't plan for special events. So remind your parents. It could help. |

Holidays and Special Days

The holidays can seem strange the first year or two after your parents separate. But even though the way you spend the holidays might change, they can still be good. Think about the different kinds of holidays: national holidays, religious holidays or observances, party days, vacation days, days off school, and special days like birthdays. Many families have certain activities or traditions they usually do every year.

After divorce or separation, some of these traditions can change, and parents usually share or divide their time with you. In many families, the parents say, *"This year, you are with me for this holiday. Next year, you will be with your other parent."* They might share the time other ways, too.

For example, some kids are with one parent for Christmas Eve day and evening. Then they leave at bedtime to go to the other parent's house to sleep and wake up for Christmas morning. For Thanksgiving, some kids go to one parent's house for Thanksgiving morning, the other parent's house for Thanksgiving afternoon. It can be fun to get so much attention; it can also feel chopped up. But kids go along with the new schedule because it is important to their parents. You might be tired of the traveling or feel happy because you have a chance to see everyone (or get extra desserts). But remember, even when you had one home, you may have traveled to grandparents or to other relatives at holiday time, too. Holidays can be overfull with activities and traveling even without divorce. Remember, you are popular with all the members of your family. All these people love you and want to see you on special days.

If your December vacation and holiday schedules are confusing or tiring, tell your parents what seems particularly difficult. Remember to keep a good attitude when you do. If you can't get the schedule changed, then try to remember that lots of other kids have had to make changes in their traditions, too.

Some traditions stay. Justin's grandparents used to visit for two weeks every summer. He was also used to lots of people at his house for Memorial Day weekend. His grandparents still visit just like before. His mom still has lots of people over for Memorial Day. When he's with his dad on Memorial Day weekend, they might take a trip, go to the town parade, or just hang out.

Gifts and parties. On their birthdays, kids with two homes may get two sets of gifts and two celebrations instead of one. Instead of one day to celebrate, it can stretch out to a week. Some kids even brag about how many celebrations they get. Other kids' parents still get together and give one gift and one big party for holidays, birthdays, graduations, or other big events, and that has its advantages, too. Everyone is together, and you don't do everything twice.

Starting new traditions. Will you feel disappointment when you can't do the same things with your family you did before? For example, maybe the Fourth of July meant barbecues, flags, and sports. Maybe winter break used to mean playing in the snow or visiting friends. Maybe birthdays always meant dinner out or a really big gift. Maybe in December you liked all the preparations ahead of time, such as stringing lights, wrapping gifts, baking, planning visits, putting photographs in cards. What can you do now that's the same (and that you liked), and what are new things you can do?

Before the separation, Daria and her brother spent the whole December holiday at home. The kids now spend the first half of school vacation with one parent visiting relatives and the other half with the other parent at home.

During the December holidays, Ben's family usually went skiing together. The first holiday after the parents' split, he went skiing with his mom and some friends. It was fun, but he missed his dad and worried that his dad was lonely. When Ben returned, he spent a few days with his dad and grandfather. It felt different, but it was okay.

Amy and Zoe's mom didn't want a big Christmas tree in the living room anymore. She got a small one and donated the money saved to the Firefighters' Toy Drive. The kids felt proud about the toy drive, but they still missed their big tree. Their dad got a big tree for his place, so they got one, anyway. Before the separation, the twins could choose one gift to open on Christmas Eve. The rest had to wait until Christmas morning. After the separation, they kept the tradition with Mom. But when they are with Dad for Christmas holidays, they get to open all their gifts on Christmas Eve.

You may want your way of celebrating special days to stay the same, but your parents may need to make some changes. If so, keep this in mind: many families change their ways of celebrating special days with or without divorce as time goes by. These new ways might happen slowly or quickly, but changes still happen. Very few things always stay the same in life.

For example, maybe a never-divorced family always went to an uncle and aunt's house for Thanksgiving and had special potatoes, pies, and a turkey. But then the uncle and aunt moved to another state. The family has to start a new tradition. They could decide to invite two neighbor families to their house for Thanksgiving dinner. They could still fix their special potatoes, at least one of their pies, and a turkey. But the neighbors could bring over their traditional foods, too. Maybe they all loved to watch football games, or play board games or video games. Not everything could be the same because they would probably miss their aunt and uncle, but getting together with the neighbors could really be fun, too.

When a family doesn't keep everything about the old ways, they can try to keep what they loved best. Then, they can start new traditions. Concentrate on what you do enjoy. Give your parents and the new way a chance. Maybe it will feel strange at first, but it usually gets a lot better after a while.

One Home

If you are living in one parent's home all or most of the time, some things will be easier, some will be harder. You can manage your daily life and schedule more easily. You don't have so many transfers between homes, and all or most of your things stay in one place. The harder part may be when you have less contact with one of your parents or he or she lives far away. You can't pick up the phone and ask an absent parent for a ride or to go to a game. Even when you have a lot of contact, it may not be in person. And you may miss living with him or her. You can make up for that as much as possible when you are together again.

If you don't see your other parent much or at all, then you probably want to find other adults in your life to be with some-times, like mentors (adults who advise you and give you sup-port), relatives, or family friends. Even kids who see both their parents can use other adults in their lives to talk to, inspire them, and do things with. Sometimes living in one home means that your parent has to work especially hard to support the family. He or she may need more of your help than other kids' parents do. Everyone needs to pitch in. This can make everyone stronger and more mature sooner, even though it can be a big change from how you used to do things. In Amy and Zoe's family, they have formed a tight family team. They work together well. Things get done and they have fun, too.

Some of our culture's most famous athletes and actors came from single-parent families. Many of them tell about how they were inspired by a parent, relative, or other important adult to stand up for themselves, set goals, work hard, and believe in themselves. Some of them speak proudly about how hard their one parent worked to provide for the family and how brothers and sisters helped each other. You may not become a famous athlete or actor, but you can definitely do your part to make your family strong and to be successful at whatever you choose to do in life.

Two Homes or Moving to a New Home

If you have one home, you may be moving to a new place sooner or later. If you have two homes now, one or both homes could be new to you, and you will definitely be doing some moving. Here are some tips and ideas for you.

Making a New Home Homey

What makes a place feel like home to you? Some kids say, "My parent is there, so it's home." "My siblings are there with me." "My stuff is there." "A bed that's mine." "I have a spot that's mine." "Furniture and things from my old home." "I helped pick out things for it."

Your bed. Whenever you move into a new place, you first want to know where you are going to sleep. When a new place is getting organized, some kids might sleep on the sofa or in a sleeping bag. Other kids might share a room or even have their own room in the new home. Daria shares a room with her brother in her new home. Justin sleeps on his dad's sleeper couch, and his brother sleeps on an air mattress. His dad says this is temporary. Ben sleeps on the couch at his grandfather's home.

Your personal space. Everyone needs private personal space for his or her things. Sometimes you have your own chest of drawers and a closet, or a part of a closet and one or two drawers. If you don't yet have your own private space, it may be that your parent is busy and forgot. You can remind your parent by saying something like, *"This is my home with you. Can we find a spot that is my own private space just for my stuff?"* (Try)

Your stuff. Daria and her brother spend about the same amount of time in each home. Only the stuff they love or need for school goes back and forth, because they have what they need at each home. If you spend more time in one home, you may also want to keep a second set of bathroom necessities and certain clothes at your other home: a toothbrush, hairbrush, special soaps or shampoos, pajamas, extra underwear and socks, and one or two changes of clothes. Words to try: *"I would like to keep some bathroom and overnight stuff here. It would be easier. Can we try it?"* (Try)

Checking Out the New Neighborhood

Take a walk with your parent and check out the neighborhood. You can get some private time with your parent and you can also find out where to go for things, what is out of bounds or best avoided, where there are bus stops and local stores. You might meet some kids this way, too. Words to try: *"Let's check out the neighborhood together. Do the neighbors have kids?"* (Try)

Having Friends Over

The quickest way to feel at home in a new place is to have your friends over.

- **Old friends.** Talk to your parent about having your old friends visit at your new place.

- **New friends in the neighborhood.** If you meet new kids, invite them over so your parent can meet them.

- **No friends?** Maybe your neighborhood doesn't seem to have any kids your age. Try to make the best of it. Remind yourself that this time is for you to be with your parent and the family. You can work on a project or homework, do things with your siblings, learn something new, or help your parent with a project. See if there is a park, community center, library, or church with activities you like close by. (Lots of libraries have movie showings, and local churches or synagogues have youth dances and weekend trips.) Get involved in a program you like at your school or in your town.

Beating Boredom

After moving to a new home, or maybe when commuting between homes or to school, it is easy for kids to say, "I'm bored." When you are bored, that's your signal to take action. You *can* make your life more interesting. You may not have a choice about where you live or how you commute, but you do have a choice about how you act about it. Look at the list below and pick at least three things you know you can do. If you write these three things down somewhere, you may be inspired to try one of them sooner.

THINGS TO DO

- **Read and do something on your "feel good" list on page 14.** This is a long list, so there is probably something there that appeals to you.

- **Find out more about your parent's childhood.** This is a great time to get curious. For instance, did your mom ever have to move when she was a kid? What did your dad do for fun when he was your age? What were your dad's goals and dreams? Did your mom get in to trouble at school?

- **Help fix up your new home.** Suggest ways the new place would feel more comfortable and then help put that together. You can decorate without spending a lot of money. If your family is on a tight budget, get creative. Lots of people find ways to be comfortable on less money.

- **Find some games** the whole family can play together, or teach everybody one that you know.

- **Learn something new** about setting up the household or taking care of it that will help you when you have your own home someday.

- **Look for what's funny or entertaining** about your situation and help yourself and everyone else lighten up about the pains of moving.

- **Sometimes doing nothing is just what you need.** Just chill out and listen to what's going on inside you.

New Rules, Old Rules, Confusing Rules

Sometimes kids have most of the same rules and routines at both homes, and sometimes they don't. Bedtimes, homework, family work responsibilities, kitchen duties, cleaning, or caring for pets can be different in each home. Some kids like the variety of doing things differently at each home, and others don't. For example, at one dad's house, lights-out is at 9 P.M., and kids have to do their homework as soon as they get home from school. At the mom's house, the kids decide when to do homework and when to go to bed. Some kids like it this way. But other kids want things to be more the same in both homes.

If you feel confused about your house rules, or you feel like giving up even trying to meet them, talk to your parent. Words to try: *"I am trying to follow the schedules and the house rules, but it feels strange. I get used to one way and then I have to switch. Can you help?"* (Try)

TIP *If your parents don't seem to hear you, look at the Problem Solver exercises beginning on page 233 and do one of them. Then you'll be better prepared to explain yourself. It could help.*

Going from One Home to Another

If you have two homes or whenever you are taking any kind of a trip (especially when it's during the school year), there are lots of things to do. Getting ready to switch homes or staying over anywhere can mean packing clothes, favorite games, schoolwork and books, sports or activity equipment, and school papers that need to be signed or shown to parents. If you have two homes, some of your clothes and equipment are already at your other home, but you have to remember which ones! Bring only what you have to—packing your stuff for traveling takes time.

Your Stuff That Travels

No matter what, kids these days have to become good at collecting and carrying their stuff around. If you are a two-home kid, you become an expert. You have to get good at remembering what to bring. You might be lugging around a number of bags when you are at school because a parent is picking you up to switch homes. There, you may need to find a safe place to store the stuff that's too big for your locker or doesn't fit in your desk or in a classroom. You've always got to know where your things are.

Even if you don't have two homes, you still have to ask yourself, "What do I bring with me?" when you go to a friend's or relative's house for a sleepover.

Look at it this way. You are becoming a professional traveler. You're an organizer. You manage a complicated life with different places to be and things to do. This is great preparation for your life. So here are some travel rules:

1. **Make a checklist and check it twice before you leave.**

2. **Have a landing and take-off pad.**

3. **Know your style of settling in when you get to your other home.**

Make a Travel List and Check It Twice

When traveling, use a checklist—either in your head or written on paper. If you don't travel much, you might be used to your mom or dad doing all the things on the list below. But if you're going back and forth, your parents probably expect you to get things together yourself. So try a checklist. You might even want two checklists—one for each home. After you make your lists and use them for a while, go ahead and add or take off things. The list is there to serve you, so it should be helpful!

JUSTIN'S CHECKLIST FOR GOING TO MOM'S HOUSE

Before I leave

❑ Water my plant.

❑ Feed the cat.

❑ Turn off my desk light, computer, and music.

❑ Remind Dad to feed my bird.

Things to Bring with Me

❏   Homework and book bag

❏   School projects

❏   Fun reading

❏   Walkman or other music player, cell phone

❏   Swimming stuff or clean athletic clothes

❏   Clothes for special activities or social events

> **TIP** *If you carry a lot of bags back and forth, talk it over with your parent. Words to try: "Is there a way I don't have to carry so much back and forth?"* (Try)

Make Your Own Checklist

Get some paper and a pen or pencil. Look at Justin's checklist for ideas, then write your own lists of things to do and things to bring. You may need to make two different checklists—one for going to your house with Mom and one for going to your house with Dad. That's okay.

Now you can make your own checklist. Use a photocopy of pages 71–72. (It's a good idea to make several copies of the page in case you make a mistake or need to make changes later.)

Then, write your list of all the things you *always* need to do or take (like feed fish or take schoolbooks). Also list things you *sometimes* need to do or take, depending on your schedule.

Once you're finished, make lots of photocopies of your checklist—maybe a parent can do this at a copy center or public li-

CHECKLIST FOR TAKING STUFF TO DAD'S OR MOM'S HOUSE

Before I Leave

❏ _____

❏ _____

❏ _____

❏ _____

❏ _____

Things to Bring with Me

❏ _____

❏ _____

❏ _____

❏ _____

❏ _____

❏ _____

brary. Every time you go from one home to the other, you can either use the same list or use a new list to check off things. This can make it easier to remember important things.

If you are good at using a computer, you can design a checklist yourself, fill it in, and print out a bunch of copies.

Have a Landing and Take-Off Pad

Your "pad" is a place in each home where you put things that you travel with. Your pad can be anywhere you put your "stuff to go," such as a corner in the hall; a hanging bag, such as a laundry bag, in the closet; a box (even a cardboard box); or a chair by the front door.

Know Your Style of Settling In When You Arrive

What do you want to do first when you arrive at your other home or at your destination? Any style is okay. It just helps to know what fits you best so you can explain it to your parents if you need to.

- **Take some quiet time.** Do you need time alone after you arrive? Maybe you want time to put your stuff away or just to play with pets or listen to music. Maybe you need to rest after the rush of moving to the other place and remembering everything. If you need this quiet time but don't get it, try saying, *"I am tired and want to rest a bit."* (Try)

- **Avoid a blowup!** Do you get confused and frustrated with making changes? If you have two homes, maybe saying good-bye and hello to parents in two different places ties you up in knots. Maybe you get hyper or grouchy just before the switch, and then for a day after. If you do, maybe you and your parent can come up with a way for you to calm down and be happier sooner each time. In the meantime, see if you can work off some of that steam by taking a run or doing some other kind of exercise.

- **Enjoy catch-up time.** Do you bounce out of the car eager to find people to catch up on their news or see new things? Maybe the change of homes feels normal to you, and you don't need much getting-settled time as long as there are people there ready to talk to you. So enjoy yourself! If someone complains that you are hyper, try to calm yourself down or do something active to work off all that energy.

Going Back and Forth

- **Traveling time.** Your travel times to your other home can be a great time to talk. You and your siblings may have your parent all to yourselves in the car. If you do, you can ask questions, talk about activities, projects, ideas, and how you feel. It doesn't have to be a time when you fight with your sibling or feel frustrated about being stuck in the car. If you take a bus or van, you can use the time to study (if reading doesn't make you carsick), listen to your music, nap, draw, or play games.

- **Feels like too much.** For some two-home kids, the packing and the traveling and the unpacking just seem too much sometimes. If this happens, talk to your parents or write them a letter about it. Maybe you just need to stay in one home for a while until you feel rested again. Or maybe there's a way to adjust the schedule between the two homes.

Ideas for a letter: *"Dear Mom and Dad, I want to spend time with each of you, but I feel discouraged and tired out about going back and forth. Could you come up with a temporary plan where I stay in one place longer, or maybe stay in one place a lot longer just for a while so I can rest up? I love you both. Please come up with a solution."* (Try)

I Don't Want to Go

Do you ever just not want to go? Maybe because you will be missing out on a game, being with friends, a party, or an activity that's important to you. Maybe you are just tired of spending so much time in the car, or switching back and forth, or packing up stuff and then unpacking it. Some kids just want a rest from moving. But they love their parents and want to be with them. Think about sharing your thoughts with your parents.

> **TIP** *It always helps to start your conversation by saying something good and true about the person before you explain your situation. For example, if you love your parent and want to spend time with her, say that first. Remember, you have to mean what you say. And you must always try to be respectful. Adults hear ideas better when kids do not whine, blame, or yell.*

Try

- *"Mom, Dad, I want us to spend lots of time together, but sometimes I just need to stay in one place. Can you help me?"*

- *"Is there a way we can change or switch the schedules sometimes so I won't miss some things that are really important to me?"*

- *"I would like to put parties and activities on our calendar. This way you will know about things I want to do."*

- *"I really want to spend time with you. But can we figure out how I won't miss so many activities?"*

Parents are busy, so they might not realize how many activities or parties you have to give up because of the new schedule.

FRIENDS AND SCHOOL

Friends

When big changes happen in a family, the time you spend with friends might also change, especially if you have two homes. If your friends drift away, don't always blame it on the separation or divorce. Remember that kids stop liking each other for all kinds of reasons. Other kids have lots of things going on in their lives that keep them busy, just like you do.

TIPS FOR KEEPING OLD FRIENDS

- Stay connected with your important friends. Look at ideas on page 50.

- Be sure to give your parents plenty of time to plan for birthday parties, games, dances, get-togethers, or field trips. Tell them the dates *way ahead of time*—and ask them to put these things on their calendar.

- Try to include friends in some of your family activities.

TIPS FOR MAKING NEW FRIENDS

- Be positive, be friendly, be fun.

- Look around, relax. Don't be in a hurry. There might be someone you could get to know in your class, on your team, or in the library or study hall.

- One day, smile and say hi to someone you think you might like to know better. Then say, "I've seen you in [name the class or activity]. I'm [say your name]." If that person doesn't tell you his or her name, don't get discouraged; he or she might just be shy. Just smile and say, "See you." Next time, smile and say hi. It's respectful.

- When you start a conversation, tell the person something you honestly liked about something she or he did. ("That was a great shot you made." Or "I liked what you said when the teacher called on you today.")

- Ask a few questions about his or her classes or interests. That usually moves the conversation along.

Choose the Right Friends

Amy didn't feel like she could trust her old friends anymore. Some girls didn't like her as much this year as last year. She didn't think it was because of the divorce, but still she wasn't sure. She felt let down. She had confided some personal things to them and now they were telling others about her. It was huge disrespect! No one wants to be lonely or cut out of the fun. But people you can't trust are not real friends, anyway.

Make friends with kids who respect you and who are loyal. Good friends can offer suggestions or advice, but they don't put you down, get you in to trouble, or push you around. When you are with the right friends, you feel good about yourself. Good friendships build you up. Maybe you teach your friend about the computer, and your friend helps you with social studies. Or maybe both of you go to skateboard parks together or get interested in performing. You can share important things with friends.

Stay away from people who are quick to find fault with you. Who needs all that criticism, anyway? People who criticize a lot are often not sure of themselves way down deep or they're really not as good as they think they are. So pull away from so-called friends who tease, disrespect, or hurt you or others. Make new friends when old friends pull you down.

. . . .

TIP *Someone who was your friend in fifth grade might not be your friend in sixth. But that same person might be your friend again in seventh or eighth grade. This happens all the time.*

Nosy and rude people aren't real friends. Friends, adults, and even people you hardly know might ask you why your parents are getting a divorce, whom you are going to live with, or even which parent moved out, or who was at fault.

That's just rude! It is none of their business. You don't have to tell them anything. Especially if you think these people are going to talk about you behind your back, just say, *"I don't talk about my family's personal business"* or *"Why are you asking me this?"* (Try) If the person asking the question is someone you trust, maybe he or she is just trying to be helpful but is going about it in a clumsy way. People can say strange things sometimes when they feel awkward or stressed, even when they mean well. Still, what happens in your family is private and personal. The big exception is if there is big trouble in your family, such as violence, abuse, or other dangerous things.

WHAT TO TELL

- You can tell people which parent you are with that day, but only if they need to know, such as a teacher or a friend's parent who is driving you home.

- Save your thoughts about your family life for your parent, your very closest friend, counselor, or other adult who is kind, on your side, and someone you really trust.

- Don't answer a nosy question unless you are sure that person is a true friend. People you don't know well who act nice can be gossipy and trash your family behind your back.

- Keep your private information and feelings inside your own family *unless something drastic happens, such as abuse or you are in danger.* Then you should tell a parent or trustworthy adult right away. Chapter 9, "Protect Yourself," talks about what to do.

Schoolwork and School Projects

Everyone who wants the best for you wants you to do well at school. But when there are big changes happening in your family, you may have to work a lot harder for a while in order to concentrate on homework and school projects.

How do you do your homework best? Zoe likes to use the kitchen table. She says that even though it's not quiet, it actually helps her study. Her parents find that hard to believe, but she gets her work done and her grades are okay. Daria wants to do her schoolwork where it is super-quiet. At Mom's, she is in her room with the door closed. At Dad's, she gets to use his den. Luke does his homework in the living room when he's at home with Mom, but he doesn't have a special place at his aunt and uncle's house.

Ask for your parent's support. If you don't seem to be getting down to the business of homework or special school projects, ask for help. Remember that parents want to know what is going on with school and with you.

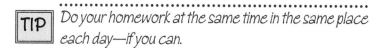

TIP *Do your homework at the same time in the same place each day—if you can.*

TIP *Do homework without loud music or TV. Homework is not the time to listen to a new album or advertisements. But some kinds of quiet music can actually help you to concentrate better.*

> School is your number one job.

Feeling Embarrassed or Different?

Some schools have lots of kids whose parents live apart. Other schools have just a few. Some kids don't want others to know about their family situation. Maybe they feel embarrassed or different. Maybe they worry that their friends or friends' parents won't like them or that they'll get picked on or teased. If you ever feel like this, tell yourself, *"My family is just as good as anyone's."*

> What's true:
>
> Your family is just as good as anyone's.

You don't have a "broken home." Instead, your family has divided and changed. Besides, anyone who puts you down because of your family situation is not a real friend. Your parents' situation is not your fault or your problem to solve. You still have a real family that loves you. All families, separated or not, have problems or go through tough times. Every family has challenges. Your family will find a way that works for everyone and that is as good or better than before. This takes courage, creativity, determination, and a lot of love. But millions of families have done it, and you and your family can do it, too!

> Remind yourself:
> I love my family and my family loves me.

PARENTS

When Parents Are Super-Busy and Don't Have Much Time for You

Your parents may be much busier now. They are making important personal and family decisions, many of which involve you. But you need them more to listen, answer questions, and spend time with you. When they don't have time for you, it's not because they love you less. It's because they are super-busy. They may not realize how much you need them. Maybe they have to work longer hours at their jobs or have new jobs. Maybe now they don't have another adult to help with the grocery shopping, cooking, laundry, and errands. Here are some ways to get closer to your parent.

WAYS TO GET CLOSER TO YOUR PARENTS

STAY CONNECTED

- **Stay connected when you are apart.** This can help you be closer when you are together. Look at the "Connect Through" list on page 50. Pick one or more ways and try them for at least seven days. Keep trying until you find things that work.

- **Tell your parents that you miss spending time with them.**

- **Suggest that you have a "date"** for an hour or two every week when it is just the two of you together.

DO YOUR PART

- **Do your schoolwork or chores before your parent gets home.** You have a better chance of spending time together that way.

- **Think "family team."** Talk with your parent about how you and your siblings can pitch in and work together to do things around the house.

- **Use the opportunity to become more independent and competent.**

BE SMART WITH THE TIME YOU HAVE

- **Use time in the car** to share thoughts and news.

- **Help your parent do something** and use that time to talk and be together.

- **Invite your parent to teach you something,** such as gardening, sewing, repairing a bike tire, playing chess, cooking.

When Parents Are Late

Sometimes a parent will be late picking you up. Things happen parents can't control—like heavy traffic, car trouble, a dog that got out of the yard, or something at work. Be patient. A few minutes of lateness is normal. Being late means more like ten to fifteen minutes late. If you must be somewhere by a certain time and you don't dare be more than two or three minutes late, ask your parents if you can get picked up fifteen minutes earlier so you arrive early. Maybe that will work better for you and your parent.

If your parent is late a lot, you can explain what happens to you. *"Dad, when you are late bringing me to school, I get in trouble with the teacher."* Or, *"Mom, when you are late bringing me to Bible study, the teacher says I disrupt the class."* (Try) Then ask them what you can do to help get you there on time.

Parents Who Reschedule

There are times when parents need to change your schedule. That can be okay. A parent might have a business trip or have to work nights and weekends. The parents usually talk together about how to make up the time. If Justin's mom had to be out of town on the five days he was to live with her, she and his dad could decide that the kids would be with her ten days instead of five later in the month or that those five days could be added during the summer vacation. It can work out great. But, if schedule changes make you tired or confused, speak up. *"Mom, Dad, there have been so many changes I can't keep them straight. I need some help."* Or, *"I'm really feeling tired. Can things stay the same for a little bit?"* (Try)

Parents Who Aren't Around Much

Kids like Ben have a parent who lives in the same area but they only see that parent one or two days a month. Other kids say sadly that their other parent shows up for some special occasions but not games or school conferences or other activities.

Parents give different reasons why. Sometimes parents think their kids will not be comfortable sleeping over because they don't have enough bedrooms. Or parents might think that if they don't live with their child most of the time, they can't be a good parent. Some parents fight so much that one of them decides it's best for you if one of them stays on the sidelines so there will be less stress. Some parents love their kids so much that it hurts them too deeply to see them for just a day or two and then say good-bye. Other parents just don't understand. No matter what the reason, you can really miss your parent and it can hurt a lot. Some parents get over this and things get better after a while. But sometimes they don't. Just remember this: Your parents are adults. They are in charge of how they act toward you. There is nothing wrong with you. He or she has the problem.

What can you do? First, keep up with friends and school and appreciate the parent you live with. If you have a parent like Ben's, look at the "Stay Connected" tips on page 81. Like Ben, you can contact your parent instead of waiting for that parent to contact you. Or you might talk to a grandparent. Sometimes grandparents have good ideas because your parent is their kid. You could talk the situation over with the parent you live with as long as you don't get yourself in a miserable middle situation. And you could write your parent a letter or an e-mail that says something like this: "I love you very much and I really want to talk and see you more. You are my dad [or mom] and no one can take your place. Also, I need your advice on some things. How can we do this? Please answer."

Caution. It might work. But if the letter or calls or e-mails don't give you the response you want, you might feel even worse. So think about it carefully. Even though you may decide to contact your parent, you aren't in control of how your parent will react. So if you make the contact and it doesn't give you what you want, remember it is *not your fault.* Don't feel like a failure. Realize that you tried.

Absent Parents

Some kids, like Luke, don't see a parent at all. Luke understands why, but for other kids, the reason may not be as clear. Sometimes "part-time parents" start acting more like "no-time parents" because they call or send a card only once or twice a year. If this no-time parent situation happens to you, or if you don't see one parent at all, this is *never* your fault.

Parents who "fade" or are totally absent have major issues and problems to work out. These things keep them from being an active parent. It doesn't necessarily mean they don't care about you. Some are irresponsible. Others may feel too guilty or too sick to call or visit. Sometimes they have the same reasons as the parents who don't see their kids much, only worse. You can be sad, mad, or even disgusted with the situation. And it stinks when you are treated as if you are not important. You *are* important! Don't forget that.

Your parent is missing out on a lot by not being close to you. Lots of kids have to accept the fact that their parent is not in their life now. They may wish things were different, but they know they have no choice. They might think, "Lots of kids have done okay with one parent. I can do it, too." Or they want to tell this parent they want to see him or her (maybe in a letter like the one above). But remember the caution I mentioned: your parent may not respond. Or he or she may answer in a way you don't like at all.

What if your dad is away for a long time, like Luke's dad? You could still express your feelings and thoughts in a letter. But instead of mailing it, you could keep it in a private place like Luke does. It would help you to get some feelings out.

Other Things That Can Help When You Have a Distant or Absent Parent

Look over the "How to Feel Better Fast" list on page 14. Are there two or three things on that list you could try? It often helps to discuss your feelings with the parent you live with or with another adult you trust. Also, be sure to read the part of this book called "Believe in Yourself" on pages 175–223. Ideas there can help you concentrate on being the best person you can be. You can build a great future for yourself with the family you have now. Set your sights on your own dreams and goals. *You are worth it.*

Too Shy to Talk

Justin wishes he could talk with his parents about different things, especially how he feels like he should do something when he hears them fighting. He doesn't know how to get started. He doesn't want to hurt their feelings or get scolded because they are too busy. If you are like Justin, try to find a safe way to express your thoughts and feelings. You can write your thoughts in a private journal. Justin might think about writing an e-mail (if he has permission to use the Internet and knows how to send and receive e-mails). He might write something like, *"Dear Mom and Dad, I have a couple of things on my mind that I would like to tell you about. I hear you fighting sometimes and I wonder if I'm supposed to do something about it. It worries me a lot. The other thing is that I worry that I'll never really see Mom again like I did before because she travels so much. Please tell me what to do. I love you both."* Maybe you are like Justin and write a letter you don't mail. Or find a kind and trusted adult to talk things over with.

> Parents are in charge of themselves.

Nobody's Perfect

Adults are not usually at their very best during separation and divorce. That means they may do and say things they didn't do before and that they may regret later. You might be disappointed in your mom because she's dating a new guy. Or you might be mad at your dad because he keeps rescheduling your time together. You may even blame one of your parents for the divorce and refuse to talk to him or her. It's okay to have these feelings. But don't go overboard, or at least not for long.

Part of growing up is realizing that no person is perfect. You don't have to like everything a person does in order to respect or love him or her. Your parents are family, and they are more special than anyone else. Parents have a special place in your life, even if you sometimes think they are hopeless in a few ways. They will love you no matter what you do or say. That's your insurance in life.

Parents Who Cry

"I saw my dad crying really hard. I didn't know what to do," said thirteen-year-old Trevor. For lots of kids, their dad is their hero and the strongest person around. When they see their dad crying, it can be a big shock. If this happens to you, try to remember that your parents have strong feelings, too. When things change dramatically, they can feel overwhelmed for a moment and they give in to their need to let it out. They may be embarrassed that you saw them cry. Or they may help you understand that it's natural to cry and it gives great relief. Either way, it may be hard for you in that moment, but after a while, it really isn't as awful as it seems. Your parent will feel better eventually. Parents need time to adjust, too.

Parents Can Take Care of Themselves

Although it's important to be aware that other people have feelings, it's not your job to make sure the adults feel happy or safe. If you do worry about your parents, remember that they are adults. They are in charge of their own feelings and taking care of themselves as well as you. You should do your part for the family as part of a family team, but this is different from feeling responsible for making your parent happy. If you want to talk to your parent about this, just be honest.

THE FAMILY TEAM

Having a Family Team Attitude

Life is a lot easier when you think of everyone in your family as a team member. Things can go smoother with a team attitude.

Sometimes your family members are all on the same team, even if sometimes you wish they weren't.

Ben's mom told him she needed him at home to watch his little sisters after school two days a week. At first, Ben was mad and felt picked on. It didn't seem fair. But his mom explained he needed to take a bigger part on the family team while she worked in her home office. With his help, they could all have family time at dinner and afterward. Ben's job was to meet his sisters at the school bus, bring them home, and help them with their homework. Mom coached him on how to do it. Ben's attitude changed when he saw how much his sisters liked being with him and getting his personal attention. They loved the high fives he gave them when they got their work done. Ben felt useful and in charge. The whole family appreciated sitting down to dinner together, too.

Building a Family Team

Maybe you have one of those families where everyone always says "Hello" to one another, smiles when they say it, and really means it. (Or maybe not.) Maybe you are always respectful, never call anyone a name, and you never, ever hit a sibling. (Or maybe not.) Maybe you usually eat at least one meal together every day, and find ways to do your chores quickly. Maybe you never fight, especially about simple stuff like picking up your things. (Or maybe not.) Maybe you try to help another family member with a chore once or twice a month. Maybe you help your siblings fix things. (Or maybe not.) Oh, well, nobody's perfect! These seem like little things, but they do have a power all their own to help bring a family together. Give it some thought. It doesn't matter if you're the oldest, middle, youngest, or an only child. Everyone has ways he or she can help out. If you can do some of these things, some of the time, it could help you build your family team. So what little thing could you do today or tomorrow? Maybe you could write it down so you don't forget it. Maybe ask a sibling to do something with you.

GRANDPARENTS AND OTHER RELATIVES

Grandparents and relatives will always be your family. They should always love you and want the best for you. Separation and divorce will not change that. You might continue to see your relatives about the same as before, or maybe not. Your mom may not want to be around your dad's relatives, and your dad may feel uneasy around your mom's relatives. This may go on for a while, and in some cases for a really long time.

Perhaps grandparents are upset because they realize that divorce is hard for everyone and that it might hurt you. Aunts, uncles, or your parents' friends might also be upset. Some kids find themselves in the miserable middle where these adults might even blame your mom or your dad for the split. If any of these things happen, it can stink. Your parent may not want you to see your relatives as much, at least at first. That might mean that if you have cousins, you may not see them for a while. Over time, however, parents and many relatives usually accept the separation and things calm down.

Ben and his sisters used to spend two weeks every summer with their other grandparents at their place by a lake. They loved these times swimming, boating, fishing, and listening to their grandparents' stories about how they grew up. They still want to go.

Amy used to spend every other Saturday with her aunt and cousins at her aunt's pet shop. Since the separation, her mom has not let her go. Amy thinks it's because her mom believes her aunt has sided with her dad. Amy doesn't think it's fair that her parents' problems keep her from seeing her aunt and playing with her cousins.

To stay connected with your relatives when you are apart, look back at the staying connected ideas on page 50. If you worry that your parent would not like you to contact your relatives, then show your parent the note, the e-mail, or the card you want to send.

YOUR PARENTS' LEGAL BUSINESS

When parents separate or divorce, there are legal things they have to do. If they also go to court before a judge, it's not because they did something wrong. It's just the way the law works. Your parents have to follow the laws for separation or divorce, just like people who want to get married must follow the laws to get a marriage license. Making plans for the "care and custody" of children is one of the laws they have to follow. It all means they have to make a truckload of decisions! People need to have all these decisions written down and approved by the court before they can get a legal divorce. They can do this by themselves or with the help of lawyers or mediators.

Amy started asking her parents many questions about separation and divorce. Their answers helped her understand why her mother was so busy and going to so many meetings. Zoe wasn't interested in learning about it. She just wanted to know where she was going to live and what days. If you are more like Amy, read on. If you are more like Zoe, just skip this part.

Things Parents Have to Do for the Family

- **Parents have separation and divorce homework.** Divorce "homework" is all the learning, reading, thinking, and talking that parents have to do for the court. The homework is needed in order to fill out a ton of required legal papers. It helps your parents make good decisions about what's best for you and everyone's future. It is a lot like studying for a bunch of different tests. Parents have research to do. They think about keeping everyone in the family healthy and growing up well. They talk to experts, read, consult the law, and get advice so they can make good decisions. All these legal papers they have to prepare and file can keep them busy for months.

- **Parents are looking for ways to agree on important decisions.** The homework prepares your parents to make the best decisions. Sometimes, when parents disagree on something (for example, on how to divide some property or belongings), they may have special meetings with their lawyers and other experts to look for ways to agree. Often parents see a *mediator* to find a solution. If that doesn't work, they may have to work with a child custody evaluator. Or they may talk to a judge.

- **Parents must make the right plan for your family.** Your parents' job is to make a plan that they think is best for you and your family. Their plan and how it will work will not be exactly like those in another family. Every family and every person in it is different. Probably, there will be a lot of things that are either a little bit different or very different. This is normal.

- **Parents have papers to fill out, meetings, and court appearances.** Your parents may be doing all of these things. And while they are, they are thinking of your best interests. This is true even if all you see is that they don't have as much time for you.

LEGAL WORDS YOU MAY HEAR AND WHAT THEY MEAN

- *Custody, parenting plan* is how much time you spend with each parent, who is responsible, and how your parents will look out for your health, education, activities, and welfare.

- *Child support* is the money one parent pays to the other for support of their children.

- *Court people* are judges, mediators, court counselors, and guardians ad litem.

- *Lawyer* is an expert in the law and how courts work. A lawyer advises a person on what is best, takes care of the court papers, and helps parents make decisions.

- *Court evaluator or investigator, court counselor.* When parents cannot agree about what is best for their child, these people often meet with parents and sometimes children. They will then tell the judge what they think will work best for the child and the family.

- *Mediator* is a person who does not take sides and who meets with your parents, usually without the lawyers. The mediator helps people think about what they want and find ways they can both agree.

Questions and Answers about Court

Will my parents talk to a judge?

It depends. If people agree, they might not even have to go into the courtroom at all. The judge can read their agreement privately and approve it. Other times, parents appear in the courtroom before a judge because they can't agree on something by themselves or some other reasons, and the judge may make some of the decisions for them. If your parents do go before the judge, you should know that family court is *not* like the court you see on TV. Real family court is quiet, people are respectful. Each person and the lawyers have a chance to speak.

How long does it take to get a divorce?

Every divorce is different. There is the time it takes to do all the legal homework and the time it takes to finish with the court responsibilities. Parents can get a legal divorce in a few months, but only if they have all their legal business homework done even before they go to court. Most divorces take between twelve and twenty-four months because the legal homework takes a long time and so does the court. Some divorces might take longer. It all depends on what the law says in your state, how quickly the court works, and how long it takes your parents to make the necessary decisions. Sometimes people have done all of their homework, are well prepared, and agree on most things before they even go to court. Other times, things are complicated and it takes a few years. A few parents have disagreements that keep them going back to court for a longer time.

Do kids go to court?

Sometimes, but not usually. If your parents can't agree on the best plan for you, the judge may order them to meet with a mediator. Or the judge may listen to both sides and then make the final decision. When that happens, *only then* may a judge want to talk with the children. This does not happen very often.

Can kids talk with a mediator by themselves?

Sometimes, yes. When parents have selected a mediator who doesn't work for the court, the kids can ask for a time to talk and it might work out. Mediators at the court may spend a little time with the kids alone. In some courts, mediators may not see or talk to the kids at all. Either way, you can still tell your parents you want to talk to the mediator and then see what happens. If you have your own attorney or counselor, tell them you want to talk with the mediator.

How old do you have to be before a judge listens seriously to a kid?

A judge who talks with a child of any age will usually listen very carefully. A judge's job is to get as much information as possible and then make decisions for you and your family. Judges might just ask, "How are things going?" Or they may ask easy questions like: "Who are the people in your family? When do you live with each parent (or grandparents or other relatives)? Who helps you with homework? Where are you after school? How do you keep in contact with your parents?" Just answer any question honestly. If you want, tell the judge things such as why you want to go to a certain school or why you would like to spend more (or less) time with a parent. Be sure to tell about anything that worries or scares you. But, even though a judge will listen carefully, that doesn't mean the judge will do what you want.

Sometimes kids won't say how they really feel because their parents told them what to say to the judge. Or kids don't say what they think because they don't want to be put in the middle, hurt a parent's feelings, or get their parent in trouble. Some kids worry they will get in trouble if they tell what they really think. If you talk to a judge, it is important that you tell the judge the truth. You can even make some notes of stuff you want to be sure to say. Just remember, it's the judge's job to make decisions for you and your family based on what a lot of people say, not just what kids say. *The judge won't tell anyone what you said.*

Is there a legal age a kid can stay home alone or babysit?

A few states have a law that gives an exact age (usually age fourteen, but that may not be true where you live. Most states say that no matter what the age, kids are not to be left alone or left to babysit if the situation is risky or there are very young children to care for. For example, Olivia is fourteen and really smart about things. But, her mom doesn't want her to stay home alone or babysit. Her mom says the neighborhood is unsafe. In another family, Dad stays home because a younger sister or brother is sick. Or maybe a parent won't let you take care of a little sister or brother because he or she is hard to handle or there is a bigger sibling who can't wait to punch you after your parent leaves. If you do stay home alone or babysit but you don't feel safe or okay about it, tell a parent. It's the adult's job to think about what is best for everyone.

Can I refuse to go to my other parent?

If there is a legal parenting plan or court order that says you are to be with a parent at a certain time, that parent is in charge and makes decisions for you during that time. If you want to make a change, talk it over with your parents. But, if the reason you don't want to go is because you don't feel safe with the other parent or in the other home, that's different. Immediately tell the parent you trust or another adult why you don't want to go. You should not have to be any place where you are in danger.

Is there a difference between separation and getting a divorce?

Yes. Separation is when parents no longer live together. Divorce is when they legally end their marriage. Legal separation is when one or both parents file a paper that says that they are no longer living together. Some separated parents decide they need a "time-out" from one another. They hope that living apart will help them solve their problems.

So then what is different with divorce?

Divorce is where married people file legal papers that say they want to end their marriage. Before the court will grant them their divorce, parents must make many big decisions about how to still be good parents and do what's best for you. They have to show the court how they will take care of you and when you will be with each parent. This is called a Parenting Agreement or Plan. Some of the other things involved in divorce papers include decisions about property and money.

What if my parents lived together but weren't married?

When parents who were not legally married decide to separate, they don't have to get a legal separation or a legal divorce. But the law still wants them to make many of the same decisions that married people do when they divorce. They usually still have to complete some of the same papers for the court, such as parenting agreements.

It can take a lot of time to make all the changes that we have been discussing in this chapter. You may have new house rules, a second home, new routines and schedules, maybe a new home or new school. For a few kids, these things may change more than once. It can be a big job, and there may have been some hard times. It's no surprise that your feelings can still be intense sometimes. But the more you get on with your life, the easier the changes seem to become. You've come this far, so give yourself a high five.

Give yourself a break from thinking about divorce and changes. Go have some fun! Later, you can take a look at the next chapter, "New Ways." It has more life skills you can use to succeed in life.

Every day I can find ways to feel more and more comfortable with the changes in my life.

Chapter 3

New Ways

Finally! You have reached the place of New Ways. You and your parents are probably more relaxed and settled down. This is a great time to explore different ways to tackle disagreements or problems in a step-by-step way. You can use what you learn to become an ace problem solver. You also might be interested in what to do when a parent dates.

Even though you may still feel sad sometimes and miss your old life, these feelings come and go faster than before. A few kids still hope that one morning they will wake up and everything will be back the way it used to be. But your new life isn't a dream, and you need to accept that. Let's look at what's new.

NEW WAYS FOR PARENTS

It's not unusual for one or both of your parents to be doing some different things from before.

Ben's dad is much more occupied with computers now than he was when he was married to Ben's mom. He uses the dining room at Ben's grandfather's apartment almost like a computer repair shop. Neither he nor Ben's grandfather mind a little messiness, and Ben feels comfortable there. Dad is showing Ben how to build his own computer and teaching him and his sisters how to use different computer programs.

Ben's mom has some new house rules. Now she expects the kids to be neater than before. Everyone has his or her share of things to do to keep the household running. There is even a chart where everyone's work is marked.

At first, Ben thought his father's computer stuff and his mom's household chores were a pain and even ridiculous. But slowly that changed. Ben now enjoys the computer projects with his dad. His dad is happier and more fun to be with, too. At his mom's, Ben admits that he feels differently about his house now that he is partially responsible for it. It's easier to find things. And it is also easier to take care of his sisters after school with the new house rules. He can just say, "It's the house rules," when they have to do something. He likes knowing what he's supposed to do, and he takes pride in doing it.

Luke's mom used to stay home. Now she has joined a church, is a baseball team parent, and attends a group with other parents who are going through divorce. A few times, he and his mom went to a meeting, where he met other kids who also had absent parents. Luke likes the changes. He really likes his mom being at all his games and helping with things like uniforms.

YOU CAN BECOME AN ACE SOLUTION FINDER

In any family or relationship, there are always some disagreements or problems, especially when people have to adjust to new ways of doing things. There are the everyday things like persuading your parent you really need the newest training shoes or arguing with your siblings about who gets to keep a pet in their room at night. There also are big things, like failing in some classes or convincing your parent to enroll you in a different school or summer camp. The secret to solving many disagreements or figuring things out is to work with just one little piece of a problem at a time. Then take another piece and work on that. Piece by piece you move toward a solution. Learning how to do this will help you your whole life!

> Become an ace solution finder.
>
> This will train your brain for success and happiness.

Disagreements, especially with people you live with, are normal. Ace solution finders discover ways to work out disagreements so everyone feels pretty good about how things turned out in the end. This means they figure out how everyone can "win" something instead of only one person winning and the other person losing. Finding solutions is no big mystery, but just like learning a sport or a new language, it takes practice. Here are two ways to try: "Cool Listening" and the

"Six-Step Solution." A third way, "Prize Puzzle Pieces," is in the "Extras" section at the back of this book.

Working Out Disagreements with Cool Listening

Two brothers, Sam, age ten, and Barry, age eleven, are arguing over where their dog should sleep at night. They quickly work out something that will satisfy both of them by using Cool Listening. This kind of listening helps each of them feel appreciated. It feels fair.

COOL LISTENING

1. **You have to *really* listen to the other person, and the other person has to listen to you.** You have to stay cool and not interrupt each other. It will go faster if you write down each person's answer.

   - **Person A tells his side.** *"I feed the dog and he loves me best anyway, so he should sleep with me on my bed."* Person B listens carefully, with no interrupting at all.

   - **Person B says what he heard.** Not whether he agrees or not, but just playing back what Person A said. No fair saying, *"I heard you, I understand."* It needs to be what he thinks the other person said. *"Okay. You said that the dog loves you best. Did I get it all right?"*

   - **Person A corrects the listener.** *"You forgot to say that I feed the dog, and that's one of the reasons why he should sleep with me."* Once you have corrected Person B, don't say anything more, just switch sides.

- **Person B gets to tell his side.** *"I take the dog out for a run and clean up after him every day, and I don't think the dog just loves you. He loves me, too."*
- **Person A is now the listener and plays it back.** *"You say the dog loves you, too. Did I get that right?"*
- **Person B corrects Person A.** *"You forgot to say that I also take the dog out for a run and clean up after him every day."* Then he stops talking.
- **Each person now is sure that the other person heard him correctly because they each played it back and corrected the other.** <u>Feeling that the other person has heard you is the biggest key in solving disagreements.</u> You can do this part of the exercise in writing. Both people look at what's written and make sure that it is correct. Now you are ready for the next step.

2. **Both people make a list of solutions.** Put a star or a circle around the ideas that each of you likes the best. Sam and Barry's joint list said:
   - I want the dog to sleep with me.
   - I want the dog to sleep with me, especially on the days we are with Mom.
   - I want the dog to sleep with me as many days as he sleeps with you.
   - The dog can sleep with you all the time if you feed him, take him out for his walks, and clean up after him.

3. **Talk about each of the ideas.** Look at each one from the point of view of how it could satisfy both people and give everyone something that he wants. The kids realized

they both loved the dog and that they both took care of the dog. Because they had really listened to each other, they came to understand that the dog belonged to both of them. They also realized that neither of them wanted to take care of everything for the dog.

4. **Choose at least one idea from your list and try it out.** The kids decided that they would try a plan where the dog slept with each of them every other night. The kids have reached an agreement. But because they took the time to *really listen to everything each of them said,* there is *also greater respect for each other.*

TIP

For your first try with Cool Listening, it can help to have a friend, older sibling, or a parent who can act as a referee. This person has to be fair to make sure both people stick to the rules so they really hear each other and don't start fighting again. After you do all the Cool Listening steps a few times, you will have started training your brain to listen better and help others listen to you.

Bigger Problems?

Some situations are more complicated, and sometimes the consequences can be serious. Here is where the Six-Step Solution comes in handy. You can use these six steps to understand a situation, help you make decisions, or solve a problem. You need a pencil and paper to do this and it will take more time than Cool Listening, but it is usually worth the effort.

SIX-STEP SOLUTION

1. **Nail it with words—three ways.** *(Write your answers.)*

   a. What is my situation?

   b. What is my goal?

   c. What's standing in my way?

2. **Think about what could happen.**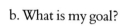

   a. What could happen if I reach my goal?

   b. What could happen if I don't reach my goal?

3. **Search for ideas to get around what's standing in your way.**

4. **Look at each idea closely.** For each idea, ask yourself, "If I choose this idea, what might happen?"

5. **Choose one or two of the best ideas.** Then start working on one or both of them.

6. **Review.** After you've given your idea a chance to work, ask yourself, "What's working well? Should changes be made?"

....

 In the "Extras" part of this book, there is a Six-Step Solution form you can copy and then try for yourself.

Luke Solves a School Problem with the Six-Step Solution

Luke's middle school classes are a lot harder this term. He's been spending a lot of time practicing and playing baseball instead of studying. Now he realizes he might fail two of his classes. He says he can't study or remember things. Although he says he doesn't care about his grades, deep down he does. Here's how he took apart his problem and found a solution.

1. **Nail it with words—three ways.**
   What Luke wrote:

   a. What is my situation? I'm failing in two classes.

   b. What is my goal? I want two strong C grades or better.

   c. What's standing in my way? I can't study. I can't remember things. (Luke's answers here will be used in step 3 below).

2. **Think about what could happen.**

   a. What could happen if I reach my goal? Luke had to think hard about this. If he made Cs, he could have the summer he wanted, and his mom would be proud of him.

b. **What could happen if I don't reach my goal?** Luke knew that if he failed the classes, he would have to go to summer school. That meant no time with his uncle this summer at the lake with friends. The consequences stunk. He realized it was better to get Cs now.

3. **Search for ideas to get around what's standing in your way.** Luke has two things standing in the way of his goal: he says he can't study and he can't remember things. So Luke gets creative! He is not a big talker, but he made himself ask three people for their ideas about how to study and remember things. He wrote them all down, even the ones he didn't think would work.

   The advice he got was:

- Study with a good student.

- Get a tutor.

- Ask the teacher what to do.

- Never lose your class notes or textbook.

- Turn in your homework on time.

- Turn down the music.

- Do your homework first, before anything else.

- Ask your parent to help.

Luke also added his own:

- Find a good place to study.

- Write down assignments in a notebook.

- Promise myself an awesome reward when I get Cs.

4. **Look at each idea closely.** For each idea, ask yourself, "If I choose this idea, then what might happen?"

   For *"Study with a good student,"* Luke wrote, "I have to find somebody good in these subjects who would agree to study with me. We might like each other, and I could make a new friend out of it. I could learn something. Or maybe we'd just goof off."

   For *"Ask the teacher what to do,"* Luke wrote, "I don't know how to talk to her. If I could talk to her, she would know exactly what I need to do, and she would see that I am really trying. This would work if I knew what to say."

   For *"Ask your parent to help,"* Luke wrote, "If I asked Mom, I know she would help. She would also know that I am trying."

   After Luke looked closely at the ideas, he realized two things. First, in order to pass these classes, he had to get his mom and teachers on his side. Second, he still had to learn how to study and remember. Luke knew that the rest of the ideas on how to study were probably good. He decided he would try most of them.

5. **Choose one or two of the best ideas.** Then start working on one or both of them. Luke chose to talk to

both his teachers. He asked his mom and uncle to help him with what to say. First he told each teacher something true and nice about the class. Then he said, "I would like to do better in this class. I want to get at least a C. What do you suggest I do?" Both teachers were encouraged by his interest. They explained exactly what he needed to do. Luke started to feel better. Now he had to start studying and remembering. He picked another idea and asked his mom to help him set up a study schedule.

Having a routine made him feel more serious about his schoolwork. Not running away from it all made him a little calmer.

6. **Review.** After you've given your idea a chance to work, ask yourself, "What's working well? Should changes be made?" After a week, Luke looked at how well he was doing. He was keeping to his study schedule, but remembering things for tests was not going very well. He went back to his "idea list" and had to admit that his new study schedule wasn't enough. He needed more help, so he talked with his mom and his uncle. They got him a tutor. Luke was grateful for the special instruction. Luke is doing the best he can. Luke's efforts are paying off. His mom, his uncle, and his teachers know that he is sincerely trying to get Cs. Their support helps Luke stay on track. Everyone knows he has thought things through. Adults respect that in a kid a lot. Another good thing is that he feels more confident about solving problems in the future.

> When you think things through, adults can have a deeper respect for your determination. They can be more willing to support you to reach your goals.

Practice solving problems in a step-by-step way like Cool Listening or the Six-Step Solution, or the Prize Puzzle Pieces in the "Extras" section at the back of this book. You might like one of these problem solvers better than another, or you might use different ones at different times. You might use some of the steps in a problem solver but not others. Sometimes a few steps help, but usually you have to do them all for the best chance to be successful. Of course, these problem solvers can't work all the time with everything, but they are a good way to train your brain to "think smart" about situations. Figuring out how to solve a problem, look at a situation, or handle a disagreement is at the top of the list when it comes to getting ahead in life and making and keeping friends.

TIP *When you want to make a request or suggest solutions to an adult, pick the best possible time to talk.* It can be any time the other person is not hungry, tired, or rushed. It can be while you are both working in the kitchen, washing the car, or driving somewhere together. If those times don't seem right, you might write it out and send an e-mail, a note, or a letter. Or you can talk on the phone. Just remember, grab your best attitude and keep it on while you talk.

PARENTS GOING OUT AND DATING

After your parents separate, they need time to get used to being unmarried. Going out is one way to do this. If you spent a lot of time with a friend and then that person moved away, wouldn't you feel lonely and eventually want to make other friends? It's something like this with your parents. Your parents might still do things together because of you, but they won't do them as husband and wife. That means they don't go out together alone or share private moments anymore.

When parents spend time with other adults, it helps them put their separation and divorce behind them. Even though they may be sad about the separation, they also need to look to their future. If you feel upset when your parents go out, try to remember that it doesn't mean they love you less or are turning their back on you. Just like you, your parents need friends their own age.

Stay at Home

Some parents have times when they don't want to go out with friends much and instead spend almost all their free time at home or doing things with their kids. Some parents may go out for a while but then spend weeks or months staying home. Everyone is different. There is no one way for them to get used to being "unmarried." Every parent finds his or her own way.

Dating

Dating is when two people have some interest or romantic feelings for one another and they go out together, usually by themselves. They go out to dinner, on a hike, to a movie. It doesn't mean that they are going to get married. The word "date" can also mean: "Jeff was Mom's date for the party," or "Dad has his monthly golf date with friends," or "My sister has a sleepover birthday party date this weekend." So some dates are romantic and some aren't.

When you first see your parents acting romantic with someone new, you might feel giggly, curious, jealous, shocked, or mad. Maybe you don't think it's right for your parent to act romantic with someone new. Or it just feels all wrong. Maybe you can't explain it, you just feel it. You may not like watching a stranger holding your mother's hand and making her laugh. Some of the same feelings that bothered you when your parents first separated and divorced may come back when they date. If this happens to you, look at it this way: these repeat feelings can happen to both kids and to parents. You may have just a few uncomfortable thoughts or extra-strong feelings or a lot of both of them. They'll probably fade as you get to know this new person better.

QUESTIONS AND ANSWERS
ABOUT PARENTS' DATING

- Is my parent dating because I'm boring or a pest? *No.*

- Is my parent shopping around for another family to take my place? *No.*

- Will this person keep my parents from getting back to-gether? *Maybe.*

- Will this person boss me around? *Not usually. But ask your parent.*

- How do I act? What do I say? *Courtesy and respect always work.*

- How can I talk to my parents about their dating? *Read some ideas from Words to Try on pages 116 and 117.*

Daria says her father has a girlfriend now and this stranger is with him all the time. It's weird watching her dad holding hands and making cow eyes. She feels that her dad pays more attention to his girlfriend than to her. Her little brother told their dad, "You don't love us any-more." Their father told them he did truly love them both, but that he wanted to feel happy again with a spe-cial woman his own age. Her little brother started to cry. "If we don't make you happy enough, will you leave us just like you did Mom?" Dad wrapped his arms around both his kids and said, "No way! I will always be your dad and love you no matter what. Even if I'm unhappy or you are awful to me. Even if I remarry, I will always, always be your dad."

Amy and Zoe's mom has been dating. Some of her dates came to the house to pick her up, and one of them stayed overnight once. The sisters felt funny about it, especially when they woke up and their mom's date was there.

They were rude to him, and Mom got upset. Finally, they wrote their mother a letter explaining how they felt. The sisters sat down with their mom and had a quiet and respectful talk. They began to understand that Mom wanted to have a special man someday. Mom agreed that the only time they would ever meet someone new was when this person was very important for their future. They agreed that when they did meet such a person, they would be courteous and respectful.

Justin's mom often brings the person she's dating to their regular Wednesday night family dinners. Justin wants to tell his mom he doesn't want her boyfriend there, but he doesn't know how to say it. He thinks his mom gives more attention to her new friend than to him. Justin finally told his mom, "I really liked it when we had our time alone on Wednesday nights. Can you see your date another time? Can you save our time together just for us?"

Words to Try

If you have things you'd like to say but don't have the words, maybe these will help.

- *"When I see you being close to someone new, I don't like it. Can you help me understand this?"*

- *"I want some private time with you, just us. I miss spending time alone with you."*

- *"I worry about you when you are on a date. Can you call me? Can I call you?"*

- *"I need time to get used to the new person in your life."*

- *"When someone is really important to you, I want to like him [or her]. It's going to take me time to get to know him [or her], so please don't push me."*

More Questions and Answers about Parents' Dating

I don't like my mom's boyfriend. He makes me feel bad by the things he says. What should I do?

Sometimes a person knows how to be comfortable with adults but does not have much experience being around children. Try to say, "Mom, when your boyfriend talks to me, I feel bad and disrespected. He may not mean it that way, but that's how it feels. What can we do?"

My mom acts differently when she's with her boyfriend. How come she does that? She feels like a stranger.

This is a good question. You can ask your mom, "I think you act differently when you are with your boyfriend. Why is that?"

I don't see what my dad thinks is so great about his girl-friend. He seems happier, but I just don't get it.

Don't try to guess this one. Just ask your dad, "How did you pick her to be your girlfriend? What is it about her that makes you happy?"

My dad left me and my mom two months ago and started living with a girlfriend right away. Now he wants me to live with them half the time. I miss him, but I don't even want to be in the same house with his girlfriend. He wants me to act as if nothing has happened. I am really mad at him for everything. What do I do?

Wow! This is a lot all at once. Sometimes parents don't realize how their child feels. They might think that kids will get over the separation faster if they pretend that all this change is no big deal. Well, it is a huge deal. Parents have a right to be happy, but it's not realistic to expect that a kid act as if nothing is different. So what can you do?

1. Try to explain to your dad that you miss him but you need time alone just with him—without the girlfriend. Tell him so many things happened so fast that you need a lot of time to adjust and understand the changes.

2. Remind yourself that you can give your opinion, but you aren't responsible for what parents do or decide.

3. Read the tips on the next page. They can also help when a parent moves in with someone.

4. Treat yourself right! Take care of your angry and hurt feelings. Be sure to reread pages 14–16 and try to talk with someone you trust about your situation. Read the rest of Chapter 1 for ideas on how to deal with your parents and stay strong. Finally, read Part III, "Believe in Yourself," and focus your energies on enjoying your own life with school, friends, and activities.

WHEN PARENTS DATE

1. **Remind yourself about feeling soup from Chapter 1.** It's normal to have feelings about this new person in your parent's life.

2. **Be polite and respectful when you meet or spend time with any new person.** Treat your parent's special friend just like any other adult you might meet at school or at church. If you are disrespectful or rude, it won't help you with Mom or Dad, and it can make you look like a dork. If you really don't like this person, tell your mom or dad in private, not in public.

3. **Ask about ground rules.** It often helps kids and parents to talk about new ground rules for how to act with your parent's friend. For example, can this special friend ever act like a parent and tell you what to do or pick you up at school?

4. **IMPORTANT: If anyone, adult or kid, comes into your home and does anything you think is weird or wrong,** like grabbing you, touching you in personal places, or saying mean things, **tell your parent or another adult right away.** This is the right thing to do whether your parents are married, divorced, or remarried.

5. **Remind yourself that your parent has chosen this person.** Watching your parent have a special relationship

with someone new can be hard, even when you like this person. Your parent may eventually marry this person, or they might move in together. Maybe not. *But it's not your decision anyway.* In the meantime, step back a bit and give your parent a chance to find out. If your mom or dad seems happier and more relaxed around this special someone, it could work out well for them and for you.

A NEW KIND OF NORMAL

Feeling Good and Those Surprise "Creep-Ups"

By the time you come to the end of the separation and divorce journey, you will be feeling pretty good for long stretches of time. But you might have a memory or a feeling that creeps up on you and makes you upset again for a moment. These "creep-ups" are like burps of memories from the past. Just say, "It's a creep-up. I'll ignore it." Or you could go ahead and think about it or feel the feeling. Even though it may feel powerful in the moment, it probably will not last long (or at least not as long as it used to). By now you know that feelings are okay. It's natural for feelings and thoughts to repeat themselves. Feeling them once doesn't mean you won't feel them (or something like them) again. Sometimes, they need a chance to come out and get your attention one more time.

Kids, and parents, too, can still have times when they wish things could go back to a time before the hurts and the bad feelings. Amy said, "Before the divorce, my life was perfect." But was it really? Her parents had very difficult times together and were deeply unhappy for many years before they decided to divorce. If you feel like Amy, it might help to remind yourself that you can't make time go backward. But you can look ahead and make plans for your life now.

A New Kind of Normal Family Life

Even with a surprise creep-up now and then, you now feel you're living a new kind of normal life. When you are settled into your new ways, most or all of your family members accept that the old life will not come back. Adults may talk about this as "healing" or "getting on with their life."

Some people get stuck feeling sad or mad or looking for revenge, especially if they feel that what happened in the divorce was unfair. Even though they may try to let these feelings go, it may still be too hard to do. It will take them longer to heal and to reach the end of their own personal journey through divorce territory. They may feel that life has settled down but, still, they are not happy.

Most family members, though, have reached their destination—a new kind of family life. They are finding new ways to use their special talents and energies. They let their life take some new directions. You can do this, too. Believe in yourself and in your future.

> I can be proud of the family I helped build.
> We can do our part to make the world better.

PART II

STEPFAMILY TERRITORY

YOUR FUTURE

ANOTHER LEVEL

SINGLE PARENT FAMILY

GETTING TO KNOW EACH OTHER

GETTING TOGETHER

STEPFAMILY TERRITORY

Many kids whose parents separate or divorce will eventually live in a stepfamily. Maybe you are one of them (or are soon going to be). Perhaps lots of kids you know have stepfamilies, too. Some things about the stepfamily journey will seem familiar, like maybe new rules and schedules, maybe some different miserable middles, a new place to live, even a new school. You can have some feeling soup, just like with separation and divorce. But there are a lot of things that are not at all the same. The biggest change is that your parent has actually married someone new. And you might have new stepsiblings as well as a new stepparent.

No matter what your situation, being in a stepfamily means more family members to get to know, understand, and get along with. In the end, you can have more people who love you. So let's begin the journey.

SNEAK PREVIEW OF STEPFAMILY TERRITORY

Chapter 4. Coming Together. When parents get remarried or move in with someone, kids get a new stepparent, maybe new stepsiblings, probably other new relatives, and sometimes a new place to live. Kids ask, "Where do I fit in?" "Will my stepparent take my parent away from me?" "Do I have to share a room?" "What do I call my stepparent?" This chapter answers a lot of these questions and helps kids (and parents) check out what's true.

Chapter 5. Learning to Live Together. This chapter is about ways to get to know each other better and how to become a new family team. You grew up with your family, but not with your stepfamily members, so there definitely will be stuff to know and figure out. Since all families have rules, your stepfamily will, too. So, you'll read about negotiating rules, stepping around the trouble among the parents, and ways to solve problems that come up.

Chapter 6. Moving Forward. When you reach this part of the stepfamily journey, you will feel you now have your own "family feeling." But, just like any other family, there may be changes in rules, chores, or schedules. Some kids will get a new half-brother or -sister, too. That's another really big change. When a stepfamily moves forward, they become a special team. There are many ways to have a strong and happy family, and your family can make its own special brand.

Chapter 7. Stepparents and Stepsiblings. This chapter looks at the main questions and gripes kids have about stepparents and stepsiblings. It also looks at the gifts that stepparents can bring to you and your family and how to do your part. If you also have stepsiblings now, be sure to read this chapter. Your first impressions (or worries) about your stepbrother or stepsister may not be correct. That's okay. There is a handy list of things in this chapter that you can use to get to know your stepsiblings better and ideas to try.

If you want to read about stepparents or stepsiblings before you find out about stepfamily territory, go ahead and read Chapter 7 first, then come back here.

YOUR FEELINGS AND GETTING CAUGHT IN THE MIDDLE OF ADULT STUFF

If you are reading this part of the book first, take some time to read some pages in Part I, "Separation and Divorce Territory." Some things there are also true for stepfamilies. Read pages 11–16 on how feelings can affect your thinking and how to feel better fast. Then read pages 16–23 on how to use special energy and pages 24 and 39–40 on understanding parents and what to do if you get caught in the "miserable middle" of adult fights or problems. These situations are just as common in stepfamilies as they are when people divorce. There are lots of tips and ideas for you there.

SOME GREAT GIFTS OF STEPFAMILIES

- All members of the family can have more people to care about them, cheer them on, and love them. There are more people to be at your games, and go with to the mall, concerts, or the library with, help you with homework.

- Your stepparent can be another parent, a very special friend, or an "assistant parent." When your parent is absent, your stepparent can take over.

- If you have new stepbrothers or -sisters, you can grow to be close, hang out together, and help each other out.

- You learn how to respect other people's ways and how to work together as a new family team.

- Your parent is happier and feeling good about the future. This is good for you, too.

- Your stepfamily has a chance to start new traditions together that include what you loved about the old ones and new ways, too.

The next chapter, "Coming Together," explains how it all begins.

Remind Yourself:

I can help myself in lots of different ways.

I can use my experiences to get stronger and

smarter. I can figure out how to handle things

as my family changes again.

Chapter 4

Coming Together

What will it be like? Your parent and stepparent believe their new family will make things much better for everyone. You may be looking forward to having a stepparent and more siblings. You may already know the other family members well and know that you get along. Or you may not be so sure about this coming together. You may be worried that you won't like your stepparent or stepsiblings. You may even think that living with your stepfamily will be horrible and that you will want to go live with your other par-

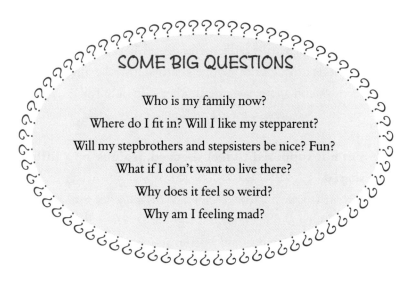

SOME BIG QUESTIONS

Who is my family now?

Where do I fit in? Will I like my stepparent?

Will my stepbrothers and stepsisters be nice? Fun?

What if I don't want to live there?

Why does it feel so weird?

Why am I feeling mad?

ent instead. Even if deep down you wonder if you are making things worse for yourself than they really are, there can still be a *lot* of "worry soup."

What ideas do you have about stepfamilies? Even if you think you know the answers, take this simple test. You can pick more than one answer if you want.

QUIZ: WHAT DO YOU KNOW ABOUT STEPFAMILIES?

1. **When people get together in stepfamilies, they love each other.**

   (a) instantly (b) after a while (c) not for a long time (d) maybe never

   If you answered "instantly," and this actually happened to you, then you are one lucky kid. It hardly ever happens so fast. A new combined family that feels like a family, with extra parents, siblings, and pets, and even new half-brothers and -sisters, usually comes after people have lived together for a long time. It's not anyone's fault. It just takes time to get to know and appreciate one another. You didn't all grow up together, so there's a lot to learn about every single person.

2. **I'm not supposed to feel shocked, jealous, or a little scared.**

   (a) true (b) mostly true (c) not true (d) *really* not true

   "Not true" and *"really* not true" are correct. It's normal to have many feelings and worries at first when people from different families start living together. It's a new flavor of feeling soup. It can feel strange at first. Or it can feel exciting. But it can still be stressful. Some kids feel a little lost, especially if they also move to a new place. That's natural. Everyone needs time to feel more comfortable with new surroundings and get to know and trust one another. There is no right or wrong way to feel.

3. **I'm going to lose my old family. I won't belong anymore.**

   (a) yes (b) a little bit (c) no way!

   "No way" are you going to lose your old family. When your parent remarries or has a new mate, things change. But it's not the end of your family! You will always belong to your dad and mom and siblings no matter whom your parent marries or lives with. Eventually, you may also feel your stepparent and stepsiblings are also part of your family.

4. **There is only one way to be a happy stepfamily.**

   (a) yes (b) no

   No. There are many, many ways to have a happy stepfamily. When two families come together to form a stepfamily, they do it their own special way.

Wishing You Could Turn Back Time

You may wish for a time machine so you could go back to when you and your parents lived together. But no one can make time stop or go backward. Time always goes forward, and there will always be some kind of change going on in your life about something, big or small.

It's only fair that you try to see how important this new person is to your parent. All of you will be happier when you eventually learn how to get along. So do your best to give it a real chance. Trust your parent. Your parent has brought this new person into your life. Maybe this person will become a big part of your family forever. No one can say exactly what the future will bring. Either way, trust your parents to do the best they can.

A New Couple

When kids have known their parent's fiancé for a while, they usually feel more comfortable accepting the idea that their parent is serious about someone new. Some kids have a mix of happy and sad feelings. You might like seeing your parent happy again, but you feel upset because it means that your parents really aren't going to get back together. Maybe you are still angry with a parent because you think that parent hurt the other by deciding to divorce. You see your sad parent still upset and alone while the parent who left is happy with someone new. It doesn't seem fair. In most cases, you have lots of feelings and questions.

Nadia's dad says he is serious about Leticia. He is moving in with her and her kids and giving up his apartment. Nadia is shocked, almost as much as she was when she heard about her parents' separation. What does this "living together" mean, anyway? She has a ton of questions.

Nadia's Questions

- Will I still have private time with my dad, or do I have to share him all the time with Leticia and her kids? *Her dad told her they would still have private times.*

- Will Dad love Leticia's kids more than me? *Dad replied, "No way! Not in a million years. No one will replace you in my heart."*
- Since it's Leticia's house, do I have a space anywhere? *Dad said yes. She would have half a closet and her own bed and dresser once they moved in.*
- Where do I fit in? *Dad said that at first she would fit in because she was his daughter. After a while, he expected that she would feel she fit in with Leticia and her kids, too.*
- Will Leticia try to take Mom's place? *Dad said, "Absolutely not. She knows you already have a mother. But she will be like an assistant mom."*
- When I'm at Leticia's house, can she tell me what to do? *Dad said he and Leticia were still talking about how this would work.*

YOUR FAMILY FEELING

Every family has its own special feeling. When your mom and dad lived together, you all had a "family feeling." Even if you closed your eyes, you knew when you were with them. There were certain sounds, smells, and moods. Like the way a sibling burps or giggles. Or the way the kitchen smells when Mom or Dad is cooking a favorite food, or what it's like when everyone is in the car together. It just feels like family.

When parents separate, your family feeling changes, too. It feels a little different being with just Mom or just Dad. But it still feels like your family.

When your parents bring new people into your family, the

family feeling changes. It may not feel like your family yet, but over time, it will. That family feeling will be different depending on whether you are together a few days a month or live together most of the time. There will also be a difference if you move into the other family's place or they move into yours, or if you all go to a new place. No matter who moves, your stepfamily will develop its own family feeling in time.

WHEN PARENTS GET MARRIED AGAIN

Your parents will decide if and how they will get married again. Some parents will not move in together until they are married. Other couples live together first and then marry. Still others live together and choose not to marry legally, at least not for a while. No matter what you think about it, remember it is their decision, not yours.

Weddings

Some couples want a big family celebration; others want it to be small and quiet. Your parent may remarry without friends and family there. Sometimes parents even have two wedding celebrations. Ben's dad and his fiancée, Tanya, took a summer trip and got married quietly without telling anyone. When they returned, they had a second wedding in the backyard of Tanya's house with the kids, some relatives, and friends.

Whatever wedding or celebration your parent chooses, you will do yourself a favor if you go along with the plans. It's important to your parent that you are polite and respectful at the wedding. If you have any feelings of anger or jealousy, try to put them aside for that day. You won't get another chance for this special event and family time. Later you may be glad to remember how you took part. And you could actually have fun!

When Daria's mom married Bruce, they had a big wedding. Daria inherited a lot of new relatives, and they all seemed to be at the party. In addition to her stepfather, Daria now has three new stepbrothers, four more grandparents, and a bunch of new aunts and uncles and cousins. It's hard for her to remember all their names. Daria got a beautiful new dress, and her brother and her three new stepbrothers all got new dark suits. All the kids had to practice walking down the aisle with their parents and standing in a particular place while their parents said their wedding vows. Daria liked being included, but her little brother was squirmy. After the ceremony, the photographer took pictures of everyone together as a new family. Daria had only one time when she felt funny. She knew it was her mother's wedding, but still, for a few minutes, she worried that her dad might be feeling all alone at home.

Feeling Responsible?

Do you worry that one parent will feel sad or left out because your other parent is getting remarried? Try to remember that adults are in charge of their own lives and their own feelings. It's their job to take care of themselves. They will be okay eventually. So relax and enjoy the party.

TIP *If you feel deeply upset about the marriage for more than a few days, would it help if you talked to the parent who is getting married? Say honestly how you feel. "I don't feel right about this. Can we talk?" or "Something's wrong, but I don't know what." If that doesn't help, talk to another trusted adult or a counselor at school. There should be a way for you to feel better about the situation.*

What Do I Call You?

Before Leticia moved in with Nadia's dad, Nadia and her brother called Leticia by her name. Now that Leticia is her official stepmom, Nadia asked her dad, "What do I call her now? Do I have to call her 'Mom'?" Her stepsisters were wondering the same thing about Nadia's dad, who was now their new stepdad. Everyone talked it over and decided that the kids would not call their new stepparents Mom or Dad until they are more comfortable. Nobody's feelings would be hurt. The kids liked that decision. Some of them needed time to get used to living with a stepparent first before sharing that special name Mom or Dad with another person, no matter how nice they were. They decided that, for now, the stepparents would still be called by their first name. After a year went by, Nadia began to call Leticia MommaLet, and her stepsisters started calling their stepdad Pops. It happened naturally.

What do you want to call your stepparents? What do your stepparents or parents want you to call them? Some families quickly figure this out, but others take a while to find the name that feels right. Many kids always call them by their first names. But maybe your parent or new stepmom or stepdad wants you to call them Mom or Dad right away. They think it will help everyone feel like a family quicker. Some kids like this; others don't. Some kids feel disloyal to their other parent if they call someone else Mom or Dad, at least at first.

Words to try. If you don't feel comfortable calling your new stepparent a certain name, say so in a nice way. *"I like you and respect you as my stepparent, and I don't want to hurt your feelings, but I'm not comfortable calling you Mom [or Dad] yet. Can I call you by your first name? Or can we come up with another name for now?"* Try

How to Find a Stepparent Name

If you are not going to call your stepparent by his or her first name, and if you are not comfortable calling him or her Mom or Dad, maybe a combination name would work. Consider something that sounds like Mom, Momma, Pop, or Dad, and put it together with a name or part of a name like Nadia did by making up MommaLet. Some examples are JuliaMom or PoppaBill. You could also use words from other languages or cultures, such as "Mamm." You might want to use a name or nickname for your stepparent that you pick and no one else uses, or hardly anyone else. Like Kit for Katherine or Ang for Angelo.

More Names

How do you explain your stepsiblings to other people? Lots of kids say "stepbrother" or "stepsister," or sometimes my "bonus brother" or "bonus sister," but just "my brother" or "my sister" works, too. When it comes to your family, you can say it's your "stepfamily" or "second family" or "bonus family" or "other family" or just forget about all that and say plain "my family." Actually, the world doesn't need to know the details of how you are related.

MOVING IN TOGETHER

Where Will You Live?

When two adults move in together, they have to decide where they will live and how much time their kids will be with them. Maybe you will be with your stepfamily more time or less time than before your parent remarried.

Your parent might decide to keep your house and have the other family move in, or move into the new stepparent's home. Maybe you will all move to a brand-new place. Parents will think about how close or far the home is from school and transportation. They will think about the neighborhood. If a stepparent had an office in the old home, there might need to be one in the new place, too. If you had a bedroom to yourself before, you might or might not have one in the new arrangement. *Ask your parent what decisions are being made.*

Where's My Bed and Places for My Things?

When you spend days *and* nights with your stepfamily in a new place, then there are more things to think about, such as your own bed and a permanent place to keep your stuff. Even though the adults make the final decisions about who sleeps where, your closets and dressers, and who shares spaces, tell them what you would like.

If the other family is moving into your place, they will usually bring their furniture, their pets, boxes of things to unpack or store away someplace, cars, and equipment. It can feel as if you are being invaded. If you move into their place, guess what? You will be the person bringing furniture, pets, boxes, and things to their place. Guess how they might feel. Often, everyone has to give up something. But that's okay. No one is to blame for the situation. There just may not be enough room for all the old things to fit in the new space. Be cool about it.

When Max's new stepdad moved into his home, Max complained, "He has so much stuff! He took my bedroom so he could have an office in the house. Now I have to share a room with my little brother. It's not fair!" Max has to make some big changes, but he's not alone. Max's brother, his mother, and his new stepdad are making changes, too. His brother doesn't have his own room anymore, and neither does his mom. His stepdad doesn't have his own place anymore. When you build a new family, everyone has to be fair. So Max and his brother worked out a way to divide the space in their room. It's not perfect, but it's a lot nicer than they thought it would be.

After Justin's mom got married again, Justin, his brother, and his mom moved into his new stepdad's house. It was a good change. The roof and windows on their old house leaked when it rained and the lights didn't always work. The new house has a nice yard and everything works. Justin and his brother still share a room, but it's much better than their old room. Their mom and stepdad bought them new furniture. Not all changes are harsh or challenging; some are a lot easier and nicer than we think. But even then there still may be moments where things feel strange or you have a surprise "creep-up."

Tips about Keeping Track of Your Things

Anytime your things move from one house to another (with or without a stepfamily), you have to decide which of your belongings you want to be sure to keep. Ask your parent if you can help pack up your stuff. Someone else might pack your clothes and books, but might not know about the other things you love, like favorite stuffed animals, CDs, games, electronics, or souvenirs. To prepare for the move, look at the following list.

TIPS KEEPING TRACK WHEN YOU MOVE

PACKING

- Ask for a sturdy box and paper to wrap things in.

- Before moving day, help your parent pack and mark some of your favorite things.

- Put a big sign or mark your name and "important" on the box.

- Take your most important things with you in the car if you can.

- If you don't have room for everything in your new place, tell your parent and stepparent about those things that you want to keep in a box somewhere else, maybe in the garage or in a storage unit.

UNPACKING

- Take your things out of the box yourself and put them away so you will know where they are.

- Offer to help other family members pack and unpack things. It helps in lots of ways. You help with the big job of moving, you pitch in, but also you will know exactly where things are kept. That helps you feel more at home.

As you travel farther into stepfamily territory, you will probably get most or all of the answers to questions about your stuff, where you sleep, and what you call each other. The next step is getting to know each other. There are a lot of new experiences down this part of the stepfamily road. Turn the page and find out how in the next chapter.

Even though this stepfamily was not my decision,
I'm going to try to be fair and give it a chance.

Chapter 5

Learning to Live Together

D uring the first months or even a year or two, everyone in a stepfamily is learning how to live together and learning about each other. You grew up with your siblings and your parent, but not with your stepfamily members. There is a lot to know. Just like you, they will have favorite foods, movies, music, sports, and hobbies. They will have things that bug them, things that make them smile, and stuff they like to do when they just hang out. They probably also have opinions about the new house rules, routines, and schedules, too—just like you.

STEPFAMILY TASKS

Here's a list of things stepfamily members usually do over the first months and years of living together as a new family.

- Get to know new family members.

- Learn how to all live together as a new family team.

- Get used to having a stepparent (and being a stepparent).

- Get used to having stepsiblings (and stepkids).

- Figure out who is the boss of what.

- Figure out which rules and ways of doing things will stay and which will change.

- Figure out consequences if rules and agreements aren't followed.

- Get used to a new room or sharing a room.

- Get used to a new neighborhood, new house, or new school.

- Welcome a new baby in the family, your new half-brother or -sister

- Have family meetings or discussions to see how things are working out.

- Learn to trust each other and help that trust keep growing.

Sure, it's a long list, but these things usually happen naturally over time. It may be easier than you think. Give yourself time to adjust and give the new people in your family time, too. The most important thing to do first in a stepfamily is to know each other better.

WAYS TO GET TO KNOW EACH OTHER BETTER

- Be respectful and courteous.

- Give everyone a chance to be heard and understood.

- Ask questions of one another.

- Offer to help each other out with little things. It's also okay to ask for help.

- Don't put pressure on your stepsiblings or yourself to like each other a lot right away.

- Don't put pressure on your stepparents to treat you like their own kid right away.

- Respect how everyone is different. You're your own person and you are unique. Everyone else in your household is, too.

Remember, even when people like each other a lot, getting along and becoming friends doesn't happen overnight. When people are respectful and courteous, the road to friendship is open. When people are jealous, rude, or snobby, the road to friendship is closed. The same is true in any family, especially in a stepfamily. Eventually you can all feel like a pulled-together family. So, no pressure. Take it easy. Give yourself plenty of time. In the meantime, give everyone in the new family a chance.

NEGOTIATING NEW RULES

My Way, Your Way, or Our New Way?

Everyone, no matter in what kind of family, has some kind of house rules. Some families have a lot of rules; others have few. There are usually rules about what people need to do for chores in the house and rules about how to behave. If you had two homes, you had one set of rules with Mom and one with Dad. Once you get a stepparent, your rules might change again. Stepparents may have different ideas about what kids should do or not do. If this happens, the adults need to work it out. Until they do, it can be confusing sometimes. So try to be patient.

Rules and Family Meetings

When a family can get together and talk nicely and thoughtfully about rules, it can really help. Daria's mom and stepdad held a family meeting before their wedding and talked about the rules they had in their first families. Then everyone talked about which rules they wanted to keep for their new stepfamily. The parents made the final decisions. The kids didn't all agree with the new rules, but nobody felt left out or picked on. Everyone has to follow the same rules now. The parents decided that each parent could remind any kid of a house rule when that kid needed reminding. Ask your parent if you can all get together and talk over the rules.

Rules about What You Do and Your Attitude

Families, schools, churches, and activities all have rules about behavior, attitude, and how to treat people. It's more than manners.

Rules can be about piercings, nutrition, carrying cash, making up tests at school, clothing choices, team membership, and just about anything else that's about you in the world. Your parents' job is to raise you in a way so your behaviors will support your efforts to be a successful and happy adult. Both your parent and your stepparent may have their own ideas about this. Sometimes your parent, and not your stepparent, will be the only one talking to you about the way you handle yourself.

Different Rules for Different Homes

Some rules are a problem. Here's one. Nadia has really different rules at her mom's and at her dad's. At her dad's, her homework is to be finished with lights-out by 9 P.M. on school nights. But at her mom's, she stays up until 10:30 or sometimes later. Her dad picks her up after soccer, but her mom tells her to take the bus home. At one home she has to be very neat and make her own lunch, at the other home she doesn't. She tries to keep it straight, but she gets mixed up and then she gets in trouble. She doesn't know exactly what she wants, but she wants things to get better. Nadia's stepmom wants Nadia to follow the rules she has for her own kids. Her dad doesn't say anything. Nadia thinks, "She's not my mom and this is unfair. My stepsiblings get to keep their old rules, I don't."

Nadia decided to write her thoughts in a letter. She remembered that people listen and understand better when you start your conversation by saying something good about them. Nadia was feeling mad about the rules. She had to stop and force herself to think of good things to say that were honest. Her bad feelings were crowding out her good memories. Once she stopped being so mad, she started writing.

Dear Mom, Dad, and MommaLet,

I know you all love me. So I'm writing to you because I need your help. The rules are really different between my two homes, and I can't keep them straight. You get disappointed in me, and I feel bad. I would like the same bedtime and homework time and rules about neatness at both homes. You decide what they are. If they were the same or close to the same, I could relax. I wouldn't feel bad about getting confused, and maybe you wouldn't get mad at me so often. I love you, and I want things to be happy.

Love, Nadia

TROUBLE AMONG THE PARENTS

Sometimes kids see trouble among all their parents. Ben now hears his stepmom talking to his mom with an angry voice about which school he should attend next year. He's trying to like his stepmom and he loves his mom. He doesn't like it when he hears they have problems, especially about him.

In another family, a dad told his friends in front of his daughter that her new stepdad was a jerk. She felt she had to defend her stepdad, but she didn't know how to do this. She felt disloyal to both of them, but none of this was her fault.

Sometimes adults don't control their strong feelings. They can say and do things that hurt others just like anyone else. If you are in situations like this, you have a choice. You can tell your parents what you heard and how it made you feel, or you can just try to ignore it and say to yourself, "This is an adult problem. I'm not going to try and fix it."

If you do want to say something, think about words something like, "Dad, you know that I love you. But when you called my stepdad a jerk to your friends in front of me, it made me feel really weird." You might ask your parents to stop. Or you might decide it's too risky to say anything and just let it go. You decide what's best. Remember, anytime you try to change how adults talk or treat one another, you are putting yourself in the middle, even when they are arguing about you. Before you decide, it would be a good idea to read or review the "The Miserable Middle," on pages 36–44.

Disagreements

Every family had disagreements. It doesn't matter if the parents are single, divorced, or remarried. For example, a parent or stepparent might want to add new chores to the schedule. But the kids might expect that things will be the same as they were before the stepfamily began. Everyone can have ideas about what others should or should not do. At first these different ideas can bump into one another. It can be a pot of feeling soup.

FAMILIAR GRIPES OF KIDS IN STEPFAMILIES

- I have less time with my parent than before.

- I'm afraid my stepparent is trying to replace my mom [or dad].

- I don't feel like this is really my home.

- I don't know where I fit in.

- I don't know what to expect.

- My stepparent or parent puts down my other parent [or stepparent].

- My stepparent doesn't understand me or appreciate me.

- My stepsibling doesn't respect me, is mean to me, or uses my things.

SOLVING A FAMILY PROBLEM

Linda thought her stepdad was fun and understanding at first. But now, a few months after the wedding, she's not so sure. This morning, when her mom was running errands and Stefan, her stepbrother, was at baseball practice, her stepdad said she had to take Todd, her three-year-old stepbrother, to the playground across the street while he worked with the family finances. Linda does not want to take care of Todd. She loves her quiet Saturday mornings sleeping late or hanging out with her friends. She thinks to herself, "Todd's not even my real brother and you're not my real dad. You just want a free babysitter. You don't care about me!" Mom returns to find Linda sulking and rude. Stepdad has a stern look on his face. Todd feels something's wrong so he's whining and cranky. Mom feels the tension in the house. She does not like it one bit. So what can a kid do? Remember the Six-Step Solution explained on pages 107–112? The family can try it, with Mom acting as a coach.

SIX-STEP SOLUTION FOR LINDA'S SATURDAY MORNING BABYSITTING

1. **Nail it with words—three ways.**

   a. What is my situation? Mom asks both Linda and Stepdad to tell their side. She writes down their answers.

   Linda: "Stepdad wants me to give up my time with my friends to take Todd to the playground."

   Stepdad: "I need uninterrupted time to go over finances and pay the family bills. She should help out."

   b. What is my goal? Mom asks each of them about his or her goal.

   Linda: "I want to keep my Saturday mornings the way they are. I need time to relax from school and time with my friends. This is the only time when I can hang out."

Stepdad: "I need uninterrupted time when I pay the family bills, and it takes twice as long when Todd is around. So someone else has to look after him."

c. **What's standing in my way?** Mom says, "Let's stop for a minute and be clear about what stands in the way of getting what you want?"

Linda: "Stepdad wants me to take care of Todd instead of being with friends or relaxing."

Stepdad: "I don't have anyone to take care of Todd on Saturday mornings."

2. **What could happen?** Mom asks Stepdad and Linda to ask themselves these questions:

a. **What could happen if I reach my goal?** Stepdad says the family's finances would get done quicker and he could get to other work around the house. Linda says she would still have time to relax. Stepdad also says that if they can work together to solve this problem, they should be able to solve other problems later. Everyone could be happier and they'd feel more like a family team. Linda agrees.

b. **What could happen if I don't reach my goal?** Linda say that if she's forced to give up all her Saturday mornings, she will feel the family is not fair to her. Dad says that, if he still has to look after Todd, it will take him twice as long to do the finances. And he won't be able to do other things around the house. Everyone says that *not* solving this means that people would feel discouraged and grumpy. It might also mean that the family couldn't work together. No one wants that.

3. **Search for ideas to get around what's standing in your way.**

Mom asks Stepdad, "Who else could take care of Todd? What other times could you do the family work?" Stepdad's ideas were that he could ask Mom to take Todd with her one Saturday when she does errands, try to do his work only when Todd is taking a nap or Mom is home, or ask Todd's brother Stefan to watch him when he isn't at practice.

Mom asks Linda, "What other times could you relax and be with your friends?" Linda found three other ways. She could be with friends Saturday afternoons sometimes, she could hire a friend who would care for Todd and take him to the park while she slept, or she could watch Todd one Saturday a month, but not every Saturday.

Later at dinner, everyone thought up ideas about how Linda, her stepbrother Stefan, Mom, and her stepdad could get to do the things that were important to each of them. Mom and Stepdad talked about things that were important and necessary for the whole family, like paying bills on time and fixing things around the house.

4. **Look at each idea closely.** For each idea, ask yourself, "If I choose this idea, then what might happen?"

Everyone looked closely at everyone else's ideas, and Mom asked Stefan to join the discussion. Linda said that one Saturday morning a month would be okay for her to take care of Todd. Stepdad said doing bills when Todd was sleeping worked only if he took a good long nap. He also said he could work some afternoons instead of the mornings. Mom said that taking Todd on her errands usually meant that it took longer to do them but she could bring him with her some of the time. Stefan said he could help out in the afternoons.

5. **Choose one or two of the best ideas.** ✓ ✓ Then start working on one or both of them.

   After the talk at dinner, the family chose several ideas and put together a plan. Stepdad and Mom made out a Saturday and Sunday schedule for doing family business like paying bills. This schedule had Stepdad's travel plans, Stefan's games and practices, Linda's free Saturday mornings, and Mom's weekly errand list. Then they wrote on the calendar when the parents would need the older kids to care for Todd. Mom will sometimes take Todd with her on errands. Stepdad will pay bills on Saturday mornings when either Mom or Linda is with Todd or on Saturday afternoons when Stefan is with Todd.

6. **Review.** [// 😊 //] After you've given your idea a chance to work, ask yourself, "What's working well? Should changes be made?"

   A month later, the family had an after-dinner meeting. Stepdad asked, "What's working well and what might need to be changed?" Everyone talked, and they made out the family calendar for the next month. Stefan said that for the next four weeks he would have practices on Saturday mornings and games in the afternoons. Linda offered to watch Todd during her own Saturday morning times and Stefan's Saturday afternoon times for those weeks. "But you owe me, Stefan!" she said. Stefan said he would pay her back in the summer by taking her days then.

Linda's family took apart a disagreement where family members felt unappreciated, frustrated, or unfairly treated. Thinking things through step by step turned the situation into something where the family could cooperate instead of complaining or finding fault. Now this family is starting to work together as a real team. Good for them! This is a big win for everyone and a big step forward on the stepfamily road.

The next chapter looks at how stepfamilies can continue to get stronger and wiser.

I can be respectful and do my share.

I can help my stepfamily become a good team.

Chapter 6

Moving Forward

By the time your journey has reached this level, most family members are working together more. You have your own family feeling. Your stepparent and stepsiblings could be among your biggest supporters in life. They may be helping you with homework. You might share clothes, music, books, or chores. You might hang out together and even know each other's friends. Or maybe not so much.

There might still be some questions about the schedule or rules or behavior. This is natural. Some rules work well. Others need to be changed. Maybe carpooling is good except for one day. Maybe you now have more homework that needs your parent's help. Maybe a parent or stepparent is disappointed with some of the ways the kids are getting along. There are always problems to be solved, and resolved, and changed again, as lives change. This is true for all types of families.

A NEW BABY

The new baby time can be exciting. If there's going to be a new baby in your family, your parent and stepparent may be talking about the baby a lot. They may be buying baby clothes, toys, strollers, and a crib, and reading things about babies. You can feel excited, too, especially if you are an only child. Or you may feel left out, jealous, or scared. Or worry that your parent won't have any time left for you at all. You may wonder, "What will life be like when this baby arrives?" If you feel like this, just ask your parent and stepparent about how life will change when the new baby is born.

WHAT'S TRUE ABOUT YOUR NEW SIBLING

- No matter how many kids your mom and dad have, you will always have an incredibly special place in their heart. Just as your new stepparent can't take away your mom or dad's love for you, neither will a new baby. If you worry about this, ask your parent. Your parent will tell you and show you that he or she will *always* love you.

- Families usually do change when new babies arrive. Babies are totally helpless and need lots of attention from parents, especially at first. Your parents may have less time alone with you.

- Families usually change daily routines when a new baby comes. Ask your parent what could happen in your family.

- Your new half-brother or half-sister will cry because that's the only way babies can tell others they need something. Crying can be hard to listen to at first, but the parents will know what to do.

- Babies can be wonderful, especially when they get to be a few months old. Then they recognize you and smile. You can feel a tug at your heart as you realize that this is *your* sister or brother.

- New babies can't talk or interrupt (unless they are crying). That means you can usually talk with your parent and step-parent even when he or she is holding or feeding the baby.

- Try to do your part for your family team. You can help take care of the baby.

- Babies learn which voices belong to their family, and they seem to know who is family, friend, acquaintance, and stranger. Babies learn to recognize the face and voice of their brothers and sisters very quickly. You are very important to them.

- New babies always need a really good sister or brother like you. You can help them feel safe and happy. It's true! All babies depend on adults and responsible siblings in order to learn things and to grow up healthy and happy.

> Watch how your parent takes care of your new half-brother or half-sister. Just think, your parent took care of you like that when you were that size, *too*.

The Family as an Ice Cream Party

One way to think about your stepfamily is to think about the beginning of your stepfamily journey. When you began, there were two families. Just for fun, pretend that each family is a different flavor of ice cream. As people get to know each other, and as respect and understanding grow, the two family flavors come together in different ways. But every stepfamily makes its own special combination of flavors. Families add new experiences and customs (like toppings). They can keep old ways and add new ways to celebrate holidays, birthdays, and graduations. They can take vacations or trips together and find ways to be close (like a double or triple scoop). Everyone can help each other out and feel like they fit in. Here are a just few versions of how the two family "flavors" can come together:

The family swirl. Both family histories and ways of doing things are important, and each family keeps some of its old ways, only now they do them together with stepsiblings and stepparent. They can become a family team that follows each other's traditions and also combines some to make new ones. Sometimes the family swirl can become a family smoothie. Either way, it works for these families.

The family smoothie. Most things about each family eventually blend together like a smoothie. It doesn't feel much like two flavors after a while, but rather a brand-new flavor they created out of the ingredients of the old ways. They create some brand-new traditions together and blend together the ways they used to do things. They can also become a family team that keeps growing together.

The family sundae. Each family keeps most of its old ways of doing things as before, but now they are one half of a new family team. When they have a birthday celebration, they do it the way they did before they were a stepfamily, but everyone joins in. One year they celebrate Thanksgiving the way one part of the family used to do it, the next year they switch. They support each other and are a family team, respecting each one's independence and style.

FEELING MORE LIKE A FAMILY

By now, your family has its own special family feeling. It keeps developing its own ways of doing things. It knows what it stands for. Each member is looking out for everyone else. There isn't one best way to have a stepfamily—every family needs to find its own way. Congratulations!

There are many ways to have a strong
and happy stepfamily!

Chapter 7

Stepparents and Stepsiblings

You know that people are different and that they have their own way of doing things. This is a good thing to remember as you are getting to know your stepparent and stepsiblings. When two different families come together, everyone has questions.

STEPPARENTS

When kids think they might get a stepparent, they start wondering what it will be like. They can even worry. What about you? Maybe you have friends who say their stepparents are okay or who love their stepparents very much. Or maybe you have friends who don't get along with their stepparents or blame them for the divorce. Even when the stepparent seems nice, most kids are going to have some big questions, especially at first.

The Gifts of Having a Stepparent

They might do a lot or a little. They could be a helper with your projects and chores. They might be a teacher for understanding

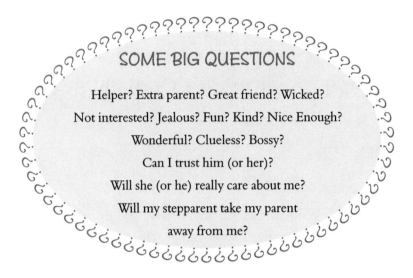

SOME BIG QUESTIONS

Helper? Extra parent? Great friend? Wicked?

Not interested? Jealous? Fun? Kind? Nice Enough?

Wonderful? Clueless? Bossy?

Can I trust him (or her)?

Will she (or he) really care about me?

Will my stepparent take my parent

away from me?

your homework, other people, or ideas. They might be a coach for your sports and activities. They can be a good friend, or another parent or an assistant parent to your mom or dad, reminding you about chores, backing up your parent, or being another boss in the house. They can help support the household with money and by taking care of things. They can root for you and become just as interested in your life as your parent is.

Stepparents can, after you really get to know them, become another dear and wonderful parent or very special adult friend. They can comfort you when you are upset and see that you are always safe and taken care of. They can be there when your dad or mom can't be. It's not their job to take the place of your other parent, but they can still come to love you with all their heart. Even if you don't ever feel that they are another parent, they could be a good friend. A caring, understanding stepparent is a huge bonus for you, your siblings, and your family. This doesn't mean that they will never tell you what to do. That's not realistic.

Justin's stepdad has three sons. His stepdad and his mom said that once they decided on house rules, his mom would enforce the rules for Justin and his brother and Stepdad would enforce the rules for his sons. He would step in only when Justin's mom asked him to. Stepdad says he wants the chance to get to know Justin and his brother before he tries to enforce the rules and act like another parent. But he wants to do things for them like helping with homework or driving them places. Justin thinks this works, and he's clear about who does what.

Now that Ben's dad is remarried and living in a house again, Ben is living with his dad on some weekends and school nights. His new stepmom makes his lunch for him to bring to school, and Ben grumbles to himself that she's trying to be his mom. But she's not. She's just doing some of the things that all moms do for people they care about.

It's hard for Ben to see another woman doing things his mother does. It's easy for a kid to find fault when you just don't want someone to be there. Maybe Ben feels he's being disloyal to his mom if he starts to appreciate or like his stepmom. Or just seeing his stepmom reminds him that his old life with both his parents won't return. For everyone's sake, Ben should try to get to know his stepmom better and be fair to her. To begin with, he could appreciate the thoughtful things she does and tell her "thank you." If he wants to make his own lunch, he can say so in a nice way.

Gripes about Stepparents

Some kids say they have new stepparents who boss them around all the time. Stepparents might say that kids find fault with them and don't give them a break. It takes time to untangle everyone's role, house rules, and who does what. If there is distrust and rudeness in a family, there are usually bigger problems.

Rebecca's dad moved into her new stepmom's house a year ago. Rebecca says her stepmom criticizes her more than ever and she can't do anything right. Her stepmom says Rebecca is rude, disrespects her things, and acts as if she doesn't exist. Her dad feels he is in the miserable middle. Maybe this family could try using the Six-Step Solution (on pages 107–112) to help get to some agreements or more mutual respect. When people are hurt or distrustful, it's the parents' job to figure out what to do to make things better. Families need to be able to live together in peace and enjoy one another.

Many kids hold back on liking or trusting stepparents at first. Often the stepparent hasn't done anything and is not at fault for how you feel. But you might still be distrustful and see mostly the negative things. Kids can really be upset for a long time if they think their new stepparent is the reason their parents divorced.

What's true is that your parents are not married to each other anymore. You belong to both your parents, but they no longer belong to each other. This means that your parents have a right to be happy with the new people they have invited into their life. But lots of kids are jealous and distrustful or feel that it is not fair they have to share their life with someone their parent picked—at least at first.

If deep down you feel that you hate this person because you want your parents back together, or because their existence makes you feel disloyal to your other parent, then be careful. Feelings of hate, suspicion, and revenge are not good for you or for anyone else. Remember, these feelings mess up your thinking and kidnap your brain and your energy. This just makes more trouble for you. Your stepparent is your parent's choice. So try to accept this and take charge of your negative feelings. Try to be fair to your new stepparent. Ask yourself, "When I really like someone, how do I act?" Then try acting that way with your stepparent. Try to get to know your stepparent better.

 The same tips for getting to know stepsiblings on pages 145 and 169–170 work for getting to know adults, too.

If your stepparent makes you feel bad or tense, that's a different story. Some people tease or say thoughtless things without meaning to hurt. They may not understand you well because they weren't there when you were growing up. Or they may not appreciate you. And sometimes they just aren't nice people.

What things are the hardest for you with your stepparent? What happens and when? Write down the worst three or four things. Next, think about talking to your parent or another adult you trust. Tell him or her the worst things. If you continue to feel bad, you need to get an adult on your side to understand what's happening and to help you work things out.

If you hate or distrust your stepparent because he or she is violent or mistreats you or another family member, *immediately* talk to someone you trust and get help to stop it. Don't wait to do this. See Chapter 9, "Protect Yourself," for ideas on how to get help.

My Time with My Parent

Ask if you can have a regular time with your parent alone every week or two weeks. It can be any time that you both look forward to and don't miss or cancel. You can take a walk, drive, go out to eat. It's your private time together to be alone and catch up.

STEPSIBLINGS

Stepsiblings are your stepparent's children. You might feel strange when you first get to know each other. You're supposed to be a family now, but you don't have the same family memories. When people don't know each other, they don't know whom they can trust to help or to be nice.

Some stepsiblings are open, helpful, respectful of your stuff, and friendly. But others might be jealous, snotty, shy, scared, and throw your stuff around. It's not a surprise that when everyone starts living together, it's a new stepfamily feeling soup! Older stepsiblings, including ones who don't live with their parents anymore, could be good friends later when you are an adult. In the meantime, you are still connected because your parents are married to each other.

If you try to be friendly, respectful, and helpful even when you feel worried or jealous, things could go better for you. Be courageous. Don't jump to bad conclusions.

START TALKING WITH YOUR STEPSIBLINGS

- Ask lots of questions about what they like to do. Ask what music they listen to, what sports they play, or their favorite CDs or subjects in school.

- Play a game together. This is one of the fastest ways to get friendly.

- If you are sharing a room, be sure to talk about it.

- Ask what it's like to be the oldest or the youngest in the family.

- Ask them about their schedule. When will you see them again?

- Ask about places they like to go for fun or vacation.

- Ask them what's changed for them since your parents got together.

- Ask about their relatives. Ask whom they enjoy seeing most.

- Give them some of the same information about you.

Questions and Answers about Stepsiblings

Because I'm a boy, I have to share my room now with a stepbrother who comes over four days a month. I really don't want to, but my mom says I have to. What do I do?
You still have to share your room. Think about how it would be for you if you were in your stepbrother's place. How would you want to be treated? What would you need to feel welcomed in the house? You might talk to your mom about what she expects. Then think about what is really important to you in your room and what should be off limits. Explain this to your mom. Then you, your mom, your stepbrother, and your stepdad can figure out how the sharing can work for everyone.

My dad and I lived together just fine by ourselves. Now his girlfriend and her daughter have moved into my

house. The little girl is always sneaking into my room and getting into my stuff. What can I do?

Even though it's natural for little kids to be curious about an older sibling's room, you have a right to your privacy. Here are three things to try:

Pay attention to her. Be interested in her as a person, not as someone who has invaded your room. Ask her about herself and what she is interested in. Your attention may be what she really wants, not your stuff.

Explain that *you* will not go into her things or her room without her permission. Then tell her *she* is not to go into your room without your permission. She might see that this is fair and the right thing to do.

If this doesn't work, then talk to your dad and ask to have a lock put on your door. When she can respect your privacy, you can invite her into your room again. Then remember to lock the door when you leave.

One of my new stepbrothers is my age, but he won't talk to me. I try to be friendly and ask him questions, but he gives me a really mean look and disappears into his room. Does he hate me?

There may be many reasons why this is happening. Sometimes kids are upset or jealous that their mom or dad is paying attention to you. He may be mad that he has to share more now or has less time with his parent. He may still be upset that "the parents" got married. He may be the type of person who needs lots of alone time, especially when there are changes. Or maybe he just warms up to people very slowly. That kind of person can be a loyal, fast friend, once he decides he likes you. Keep up your friendly and respectful behavior. Eventually you may have a friendship.

I live with my dad and stepmom and three stepsisters. My stepsisters get new clothes but I just get the hand-me-downs. I feel like I'm not important. What can I do?

Not feeling important is a miserable feeling. Perhaps there is a misunderstanding. Maybe your stepsisters get new clothes as gifts from other relatives. Maybe your dad is in charge of buying your clothes, and your stepmom is responsible for your stepsisters' clothes. If that isn't the explanation, then try this. Go to your closet and put your hand-me-down clothes on one side and new clothes on the other side. Look hard and see if you are exaggerating how few new clothes you have. If it still looks like you are mostly getting hand-me-downs, bring your dad to your closet and show him how you have sorted your clothes. Ask him why this is happening. Tell him how it makes you feel. If things change for the better, be sure to tell him that you appreciate the change. If things don't change, then bring it up again in a month or two.

My new stepbrother is fifteen and I am eleven and a girl. He grabs me, hits me hard, and teases me in a mean way. I'm scared of him. Dad says he talked to my stepmom about it, but it hasn't stopped. My stepbrother is just sneakier when he does it now. How can I make this stop?

You are doing the right thing by telling your dad. This should not be kept a secret. If you ever have any bruises or cuts when you get hit or grabbed by anyone, show these to an adult like your dad or stepmom immediately. It's their job to protect you. If your stepbrother is leaving marks or scaring you, maybe the adults will decide that you need to stay with your mom until the adults figure out how to control your stepbrother's bullying behavior. If you don't think it's necessary to go live with your mom, maybe you can ask your stepbrother, stepmom, and dad to meet together and talk about what's happening. Even though stepkids can have fights or be mad at each other, they should never hurt each other. Definitely, no one should scare or bully someone else. You need to protect yourself, especially if he does these things again when the parents aren't home.

Before my mom got married again, I was the youngest in the family. Now I have two younger stepsiblings most of the time. They are okay, but I feel jealous and sometimes mean about it. How can I get a better attitude?

This is a big change for you, so it won't feel normal overnight. It can help to think about what's cool about being older than your stepsiblings. Concentrate on the good parts. Do the kids look up to you? Do they think you are the greatest? They might be your little helpers. You can be their teacher, too. You get to be more of a grown-up in the family and take on more responsibilities. It can be good to be stronger and smarter about things. Try to look more at what's good instead of what's not so good.

Take Your Time

Your stepparent and stepsiblings are in your life now. They are part of your family and you are a part of theirs. Sure, living in a stepfamily is sometimes a challenge, but many kids eventually come to respect and truly love their stepparents and stepsiblings. So take it easy. Be patient with yourself and others. Nina grew up with a stepfamily. She said, "I am lucky to have three wonderful loving parents and two more sisters. I can't imagine my life without them."

I take pride in the stepfamily I helped build. My stepfamily can do its part to make the world better.

PART III

BELIEVE IN YOURSELF

FUTURE

BELIEVE IN YOURSELF

HAVE   HEART

GOALS   DREAMS

LIFE SKILLS

TAKE CARE
OF YOUR
BODY
                YOUR
                LIFE   PROTECT
                              YOURSELF

BELIEVE IN YOURSELF

Y ou can't do anything about your parent's big decisions—especially about separation, divorce, or getting remarried. But you can do a lot to help yourself and treat yourself right. You don't have to feel helpless—or at least not for long. You can believe in your ability to handle changes as they come along and get on with your life of being a kid. This doesn't mean that changes always feel great or that you don't get discouraged. It does mean that you can feel more confident that you can eventually find a way that works for you. Even when it takes more time than you want, you can still believe you can get there.

This part of the book has more tips and ideas on how to take care of yourself and how to get stronger and smarter. Treat yourself right. You can develop (or make stronger) those habits that keep you strong, healthy, safe, and believing in yourself and your future.

SNEAK PREVIEW OF WHAT TO EXPECT

Chapter 8. Your Body. You need it your whole life! Do you want to enjoy yourself and have the energy and strength to do what you want? Then you must take care of your body. This chapter gives you a head start.

Chapter 9. Protect Yourself. Kids have to know what to do if they have a dangerous situation in their family. This chapter shows you how to protect yourself. Even if your family does not have serious trouble like this, you may have a friend who does. It's good to know certain information anyway.

Chapter 10. Have Dreams and Goals. Forget about troubles! What about your wishes and dreams? This chapter shows you a step-by-step way you can start making those wishes actually become real. It's called "power daydreaming," and you can start right now.

Chapter 11. What's True about Life. This chapter has even more ways to train your brain to get rid of that negative thinking or feeling like a victim. There are more ideas on how to get stronger and happier and how you can repair bad choices. Find out about "body smarts" and some tips about your feelings including those that can get you into trouble.

Chapter 12. Believe in Yourself. This is the last chapter in the book. It talks about having heart, believing in yourself, and having a successful and happy life.

GROWING UP

Growing up always means discovering how to develop good judgment and make wise choices for yourself and others. No one anywhere has a perfect life, and everyone everywhere has to make changes and meet challenges. This is one of the facts of life. The key is to find ways to get stronger and smarter because of what you experience no matter what happens. Why not use your experience to help build yourself up so you can be in better shape than when all these changes started? You have to go through the family changes anyway. Why not get more out of it? It's your life! One girl said, "You get experiences that other kids don't. Even though you may not like your experiences it teaches you. You *don't* want to grow up to make poor decisions."

If you do a few things for yourself every day, eventually you will automatically be true to yourself in most things.

Chapter 8

Take Care of Your Body

I t may sound boring because you've heard it from your parents or teachers, but it's true: take care of your body! Anytime you are stressed or go through big changes, it's not just hard on your feelings, it's also hard on your body. When you are stressed, it's much easier to get sick, have accidents or sports injuries, or lose strength and energy. You can get more headaches and stomachaches and miss out on parties, games, fun activities, and school, or just feel crummy. The reason you feel bad is because of the stress or a gross kind of feeling soup. The good news is that if you take good care of your body, everything can feel much better, including how you feel and think. If you also do some of the things on the "How to Feel Better Fast" list on page 14, you can feel better even faster.

> I promise myself I will take care of my body.
>
> I will need it my whole life.

HOW DO I TAKE CARE OF MY BODY?

- Good routine

- Good personal cleanliness

- Good food

- Good sleep

- Good exercise

- Good relaxation

- Knowing how my special energy works

Good Routine

A routine is a set of things you usually do to accomplish something. When you do the same things in the same way (or close to it) every day, you train your brain, and doing these things becomes easy. You don't have to think much about it. Michael wakes up with an alarm clock, goes straight to the bathroom and washes his face, then gets dressed and combs his hair. He grabs his book bag and homework and takes them down to the front door. Then he's ready for breakfast. After breakfast, he puts his dishes in the sink, changes the dog's water, and brushes his teeth. It's automatic to him now. He doesn't have to think about it much.

What do you do to get ready for school? What about mealtimes, bedtimes, chores, homework periods, and getting yourself cleaned up? If you have a routine that works for you, it's like your mind and body's secret best friend. Smart routines make your day go smoother and can give you a healthier body. If you are not a "routine" kind of person, just make sure you do find time to take care of yourself in some regular way. When you feel stressed, be sure to stick to your routine. It can calm you down.

Good Personal Cleanliness

This means get clean—body, teeth, hands, feet, hair. Some people love to take long showers, and they floss their teeth, and brush their hair. But others don't want to take time doing all that. Even if you don't feel like it, find a way to get clean every day anyway. Nobody should have to remind you. Your body, teeth, and hair can do their jobs better when they are clean. And other people like being around people who smell and look clean.

Good Food

Everybody needs nutritious food. Some people are hungry only for the right food. But most of us have learned to like not so healthy foods, because they can taste terrific. We need to manage what we eat in order to keep our body strong. Do you know that some foods can make it harder to think and others can actually calm your emotions? The fact is that the right foods make your life better in many ways. Your brain and body will thank you very much for making good food choices. So take care of your body by putting good stuff in it.

Good Sleep

Kids, especially those who are in a growth spurt, need at least eight to ten hours of sleep a night. That's because sleep is when your body does most of its growing and repair work. We all need the kind of sleep we have when we dream and also the deep part of sleep when we don't dream. So you can't cheat with sleep. It is especially important when your body is developing quickly or when you have lots of changes or activities in your life. Some kids have an internal sleep clock that makes them go to sleep when their body needs it. But most of us can ignore our body's need to sleep when we shouldn't, because we have so many other ways to spend our time. But getting good sleep is a very good way to take care of yourself.

TIP *If you have trouble falling asleep, you might need to turn off electronic items an hour before bedtime and relax with quiet music or a book. Remember, your body and brain will be in much better shape if you really rest. You'll be in a better mood during the day and perform better at everything.*

Good Exercise

If you are athletic, then exercise probably comes naturally to you. You need to move a lot, and you are happiest when you do. But maybe you are not an athlete, or you are a couch potato who feels cozy watching TV or playing a game. Watch out! Your body needs to move. It works best when there is the right kind of exercise, especially for the large muscles in your legs. That's why biking, walking, running, and certain sports help keep you in shape. Exercise can help keep you at a good weight, too. It helps you think clearly. It works off stress when changes or events make you mad or worried. So go ahead and move your body. Dance to some music. Make it part of your routine.

Good Relaxation

With all the things going on in your life, find time to relax every day. Make it part of your daily routine. Maybe you relax in bed before you fall asleep. It's quiet, you're by yourself, and no one is bothering you. It's a good time to daydream or think about your day. Maybe you can relax by doing fun things that take your mind off school, problems, the divorce, or your new stepfamily. Maybe you like reading, watching TV, skateboarding, playing games with friends, or just hanging out. Whatever works for you, the right kind of relaxation is just as important to a strong body as exercising.

Knowing How Your Special Energy Works

In the first part of this book (pages 16–21), you read about the special energy that all humans have. When the survival part of our brain senses that we could be in danger, it sends our body a signal that pumps up our energy and strength to high, higher, or highest. This special energy can help you excel in many areas once you get to know how it works in *your* body. So take care of your special energy, too. Look at the tips and suggestions on pages 19–21 for ways to control it and use it.

> Treat your body well, and it will treat you well.

Examples of How You Take Care of Your Body

Daily routines work. Justin remembers how sad he was when his grandfather died. He missed him and he grieved. But his mom made sure he still went to school and kept to his regular routine anyway. He got lots of rest and ate good food. He learned that even when things are really hard, a routine, the right foods, and plenty of sleep can help you handle your feelings better.

Preventing pain. Ben kept forgetting to brush and floss. It seemed like too much trouble. Eventually, he got cavities and gum problems. That meant many trips to the dentist with shots and fillings. If he had made the effort to remember to care for his teeth, he might have avoided this pain.

Getting more oxygen. When Zoe and Amy started biking to school, they were much more alert in class and remembered more. They didn't have to study as much. They were getting more oxygen to their brain because they were exercising.

Taking a break. Luke was fed up. He felt like he was surrounded by too many new things he was supposed to do. He decided to just relax for a while every day right after school or practice. By doing nothing special, he gave himself a break.

This chapter has covered the basics of your body. The next chapter is about protecting yourself and your body if you have serious trouble in your family.

When I take care of my body, I am respecting myself and treating myself right.

Chapter 9

Protect Yourself

There are plain old everyday problems in families, and there are *really big problems where something is happening in your family that puts you or others in danger.* Big problems are very different from everyday problems. Everyday problems happen in all families. For instance, when parents are irritable, crabby, and just not acting like themselves because of worry or illness. Maybe a parent is working extra hours and you have pizza or snack food for dinner a lot. Or your parent is sad and spending more time alone but still manages to take care of you. Maybe a parent screams at you and grounds you for a month or your bigger brother or sister shoves you around and calls you a loser. Nobody likes to be treated like this, but, as unhappy or angry as this makes you feel, your life is not in danger. *Everyday problems are NOT what we are talking about in this chapter.*

This chapter is for kids who are in real danger because they have parents, family members, or other adults in their lives with really big problems. These kids never know when something truly awful is going to happen or what danger they'll find when they get home. Or they are so scared or worried about being with the other parent that it is always on their mind. Here are some examples.

SOME REALLY BIG PROBLEMS

- If you or a family member is getting punched, hit, pinched, slapped, shoved, or beat up. Or you are told that these things will happen to you. This is called "domestic abuse" or "domestic violence." This is against the law. Kids should be safe with their siblings and adults, and adults should be safe with each other.

- If someone has a weapon and threatens you or another family member with it. These threats are against the law. And they are very dangerous.

- If you feel that something is really wrong with a family member. Maybe you don't know what it is, but you feel it. Maybe that family member is sick, zoned out, or acting so strange that he or she cannot take care of you. You may not be in danger, but this person might need help.

- If your parent has friends around who really scare you. Maybe they do irresponsible things like using drugs. This could be dangerous. They are not using good judgment.

- If any adult, sibling, or stepsibling touches you in private places or tries to do this, this is wrong. No one should *ever* do that to a kid. It is also against the law for anyone to do this to a kid.

- If you don't get enough food to eat or a clean place to sleep or live because a parent neglects you. This is unhealthy for you, and it is against the law for children to be treated this way.

- If a family member is hurting himself or herself by making him or herself throw up, refusing to eat, or cutting his or her body, this person is suffering. This may not be dangerous for you, but it is dangerous for that family member. It is also unhealthy for the whole family.

If none of these things is happening to you, you may want to skip this chapter. But if these things are happening to you or to a friend, read on. You can also share this chapter with him or her.

SECRETS

Sometimes people tell a child to keep secret the bad things that are happening. That makes it hard to figure out what to do. Kids may feel embarrassed or sorry for their parent or that person. They might feel disloyal even thinking about telling anyone about what's happening. They may also be afraid that this person will hurt them or threaten them if they do tell someone.

Kids can also worry that an adult outside of the family they tell about the trouble won't believe them. But when kids are in real danger, they have to at least think about how to get safe and stay safe. Anyone outside the family whom you tell has a legal responsibility to get someone to protect you, but people don't always believe what kids say. Some kids don't want to tell because they don't know if that person will go back and tell their parents or the person who has the problem. That might make things worse for the kid who told. So if you do have a big problem in your family and your parent can't fix it, you must carefully choose whom you tell. If the person you tell doesn't help you, you have to find another person to talk to who will help.

PROMISES

Sometimes parents or adults who are doing these really bad things may say they are sorry and promise never to do them again. Even siblings or stepsiblings who are doing something to you may make promises. They probably mean what they say, but they may not be able to help themselves, and they do these bad things again later. It's not easy to know what to do. For example, what if your dad came over to your house and hit your mom whenever he got really mad? But this time, your mom called the police. Your dad might tell you to lie to the police or a court person about what really happened. *Don't do it.*

- Don't lie about what happened, just tell the truth.

- If you are afraid of what will happen if you tell the police or court person, be sure to explain this first. Ask what will be done to keep you safe, *starting right now before you tell.*

- You are not guilty or disloyal. This is not your fault.

- Remember, you and the rest of your family need to be safe! And the family member who is causing the problem needs help to change.

When people who hurt others are serious about changing their awful behavior, you will know it's true because they go to get help to change immediately. And they don't ask you to lie. But some adults with serious problems believe they don't need help and think other people are against them. Sometimes adults don't know where or how to get help. Or maybe they don't think getting help will work. This makes it hard for them to change unless the law or another adult forces them. Then, once the law makes them get help, many of these parents can work hard to change. They can go to counseling or take special classes to get better. Until they do, the court might think it's best that the kids see their parent when there are other responsible adults around who will make sure nothing dangerous happens.

HOW TO GET SAFE

Who Can Help You?

This person could be a parent or a stepparent. It might be a grandparent or another relative; a neighbor; a friend's parent; your minister, priest, or rabbi; a police officer or a counselor at school. Maybe you have a therapist or know someone with the court or social services. You need an adult you can count on who is on your side and who will protect you.

Call or tell this adult you trust. Tell what's happening and why you are scared. Don't wait until it happens again or things get worse. *Act now.* If the adult doesn't do anything, or is too slow to act, tell another adult you can trust.

For example, about three months ago Billy came back from being with his dad and saw that Mom had bruises on her arms and her face. She said she fell down, but she acts really afraid of his stepdad. Last month, Billy saw him hit his mom really hard, and Billy ran and hid way back in his closet. Then last week, it happened again, and this time his mom acted really sick and didn't want to talk about it. Then Billy called his grandparents, who came and got him and his mom and took them to their house. The adults are working out what to do now. It is not Billy's job to figure out what comes next.

Have a safety plan

This is a plan that you work out with the adult you trust to fit your special situation. For example, Megan's dad and step-mom have nasty fights, and her dad sometimes throws and smashes things. First her stepmom got hurt when a plate hit her in the head. Everyone acted sorry. Megan talked to her dad and he said it would stop, but it hasn't. The last two times they fought, Dad shoved Stepmom so hard she fell and had to go to the doctor. Then everyone was sorry again, but Megan was still scared. What if it happens again and things are worse? She doesn't think she can talk to her dad or stepmom about this anymore.

Megan really needs to talk to her mom or another adult. The adult needs to find someplace safe for her to live until the parents change.

A safety plan has instructions for what to do if you

think that you or a family member may be in danger, especially because of violence or weapons.

HOW TO MAKE A SAFETY PLAN

Answer the questions below. Then, if you feel you or a family member is in real danger, think "Code 1-2-3." The "Code" is a word the family keeps secret from the abuser. When the abuse starts, saying the code word means, "Start the Safety Plan."

> 1. **Get out of the house or hide.**
>
> 2. **Get someplace safe.**
>
> 3. **Get help.**

1. **Get out of the house or hide.** The safest exits from my house are _____. (If you can't get out, where can you hide? Closet? Under the bed? Bathroom?)

2. **Get someplace safe.** These are the safe places I can go.

    _____

    (Neighbor? Hospital, fire station, or police station? Friends?)

3. **Get help.** Call 911 if you want the police to come right away. Always call your other parent or another adult to help you decide what to do or to pick you up at the neighbor's or other safe place. If you have a cell phone, always keep it with you and charged.

Memorize these numbers or put them in your cell phone:

911 and 1-800-799-SAFE (7233), a 24-hour hot line.

The phones of your safe parent or others who can help.

Don't be alone with a really scary situation. Find someone you trust whom you can talk to, especially if you are scared or depressed.

> The safety plan is like a fire drill.
>
> You may not need it, but it's a good thing to have.

911 Is the Fastest Way to Get Help!

Most safety plans include calling 911. You probably learned in kindergarten or elementary school to get out of the house if there is a fire and to go to a neighbor's home to call 911. Or if someone in the house is injured, you call 911 and ask for an ambulance or paramedic. You can do the same thing if anything else really bad or dangerous is happening.

You call 911, explain what's happening, and ask for help. The police may want to come to your house right away. Remember, you can also call 1-800-799-SAFE (7233).

Questions and Answers about Big Trouble

My dad threw things and punched us and our mom. Mom called 911 and got Dad arrested. She also got an

order from the court that kept Dad away from us. Then Dad went to jail. I don't want people to know that my dad is in jail. When I get older, am I going to have problems with being violent, too?

First, you don't have to tell anyone. It's your private, personal life and nobody else's business. Second, the most important thing to realize is that you are not your parent. You are your own independent person with your own life to live. You do not automatically grow up to be like any of your parents or relatives. You can choose how to act. You are already learning how to take care of yourself in a way that maybe your dad could not. People do bad things when they feel they don't have (or know about) different choices. How to make good choices is probably something your dad didn't learn at your age. But you can make good choices.

Your mom is giving you a good example. She has chosen to protect you and herself by making sure your dad does not hurt you anymore.

My mom's boyfriend punches and shoves my mom when he gets mad. I try to stop him by pulling at his arms, but he hits me really hard, too. He told me I'd be really sorry if I tried to stop him again. Do I call 911 the next time?

Don't wait for this to happen again. You and your mom need to be safe *now*. Tell your mom you are afraid and you don't want her or yourself to be hurt. If you think your dad can help, suggest that you or your mom call him and explain the situation. Ask him to find you a safe place away from the boyfriend. If Dad can't help, maybe another adult can, a grandparent, relative, or neighbor. You or your mom can also call 911 for free from a public telephone and explain what happens. If you call 911, the police usually come to the house right away. Be sure to tell the 911 operator that the boyfriend has said you would be really sorry if you told on him and that you and your mom need protection from him right now. The police (and the people in the fire department) are required by law to get help for you.

My mom hit us a lot and broke my sister's arm. Then, Dad made us live with him. Now Mom can't see me and my sisters except on weekends at this center and not at her new place. I'm mad at my dad because now I can't see my mom much. I'm confused.

You can be angry with your dad, even though you know he was protecting you. You probably feel relieved that Mom can't hurt you anymore, but you can still miss her. But your mom has a major problem. Hopefully, she's getting help now and after a while you can spend more time together. It's okay to have mixed feelings.

My stepdad has been touching me where he shouldn't. He says it is not wrong, but I know it is. I feel awful and scared. I don't know if my mom will believe me. Is this my fault? What should I do?

This is definitely *not* your fault. Your stepdad is wrong to do this. Adults who do this to kids have a very big problem no matter what they say. First, tell your mom. If she won't believe you, tell another adult you really trust about this. You need to be safe from this right away. If the people you tell don't do anything, tell a counselor or nurse at school. Write down exactly what happens and give the paper to the adult you trust. If you know someone at the court (like a case worker or guardian ad litem), or a counselor at social services, call them and tell them what's happening. They should take action to protect you.

My dad does not make me anything to eat the days I'm with him. Half the time, he also brings me very late to school or I have to call Mom to take me because he won't wake up. Sometimes he acts so hyper and weird that I get really scared. He has some strange friends over a lot who mess up the house and look at me funny. Do I tell my mom everything that's happening?

Your dad has a big problem. Tell your mom or some other responsible adult you can trust everything that's happening. If you are ever with anyone who really scares you, go to a neighbor and say that you need to call a relative to come and get you there at the neighbor's house.

My mom has been acting really different for two weeks. She has been staying in the bedroom and sleeping or sitting in the dark. I can't get her to want to talk, or go to work, or cook any meals. My older brother and I have kept this a secret. We don't want to embarrass her or have my dad mad. We have been taking care of things when we come home from school. But now we are getting worried. What should we do?

Your mom is not well and needs help. You can try saying, "We love you and want you to be well. You aren't acting like yourself at all. You are scaring us. We need help." Maybe after hearing this, your mom will be able to tell you what to do. But if things don't get better, call an adult you trust, like your dad, another relative, or the parent of a close friend. What your mom is doing is not a bad thing, but she is suffering and you need to be taken care of. This is a job for another adult who can help.

Do I have to ride in the car alone with my mom's boyfriend? My mom says I have to.

If the boyfriend is an unsafe driver—going through stoplights, driving too fast or dangerously—tell your mom exactly what he does that is unsafe and scaring you. Tell her this is why you won't ride with him. If you have an icky feeling about being alone with him and you are afraid he might do something bad to you, tell your mom that, too, and stay out of the car. If your mom forces you to ride with him anyway, tell your dad or someone else you trust about your worries and ask them to take care of the problem.

My stepmom drinks a lot sometimes and I don't want to drive with her if it's going to be dangerous. How can I tell when to call my dad and refuse to get in the car with her?

An unsafe driver is one whose judgment and reflexes are poor. Too much alcohol makes drivers unsafe. People may smell of alcohol or look, act, or sound different. They might have a strange giggle, act confused, or be extra hyper or angry. Their words might not make sense or be sloppy sounding. For example, like "neeswatr" for "I need some water" or "geincar" for "get in the car." Their eyes often look strange. Their face or body may even twist in unusual ways and they might stumble or bump into things. They may do things slowly or act half asleep. They may not remember what you just said and they often don't realize they shouldn't drive. If any of these things are happening, call your dad or another trusted adult right away and don't get in the car.

 People who are sick, take certain medicine, or are on illegal drugs can also drive dangerously. They can act a lot like people who have had too much to drink.

REMEMBER, YOU ARE NOT YOUR PARENT

Some kids worry that if their parent is violent, acts crazy, drinks, or does drugs, they will do the same as they grow older. *Not true!* Remember, kids do not have to do the same bad things their parent is doing. Everyone has choices. Kids know how much hurt their parent's problem has caused. They know the situation is not good for them. If you are one of these kids, make up your mind now that even if you look just like your parent, you still are a *totally different person.* You can guard against having these problems. Just by reading this book, you're remembering or learning ways to take care of yourself in a way that perhaps the person who is sick or violent never learned. People do bad things when they feel they don't have choices or know how to do things differently. But you can make different choices because you're taking the time to read and learn about different ideas and choices. That's probably something the other person didn't learn at your age.

It is not easy when you have really big trouble in your family. Try to have courage and help yourself and your siblings by being especially good to one another. Appreciate and support the parent who is trying to protect you and find ways to keep you safe. It's hard to live with a parent or another person who is very ill or who puts other people in danger or hurts them. Just remember, you can't fix that parent's problem. This is a job for the adults.

> You can have a healthier and happier life and be a great parent to your own children someday.

Chapter 10

Have Dreams and Goals

A wish or a dream doesn't have to be about huge things like making a million dollars or winning awards or even about your future career. Instead, ask yourself what you would like to happen in the next year or two or even three or four years. For example, Max secretly wishes he had a few good and loyal friends to hang out with. Angela wishes she could play on the school's first-string volleyball team next year. Doug thinks Japanese is a cool language and wishes he could speak it.

POWER DAYDREAMING

Your daydreams can be powerful. They can help you in lots of ways. They can give you a break from thinking about harsh things. You can become excited about something new and positive. You can feel good while you're daydreaming. Daydreams spark your imagination and exercise your brain. They can make you interested in learning more, in trying things that make you more in charge and confident. As Marcy said, "Daydreaming makes you want to work hard at something you want to achieve. It gives you hope and power. It takes your mind off of family situations." First, you have to give it a chance to work.

HELPING DREAMS COME TRUE

- **Dream!** Wish!

- **Feel** how it would be if the dream came true.

- **Follow** the ideas and questions that come up when you think about your dream.

- **Keep a "considerations" list** of things that might stand in your way or make it harder to do (like getting permission or having enough money).

- **Set a small goal** for yourself and do things to reach it. Then set another one. Then another. Give yourself a high five or a thumbs-up when you reach each of your goals.

- **Keep piling up your small goals** until you've made your dream come true (or something just as good). Give yourself a reward for getting there.

> Give your dreams a chance!

LEARN HOW TO BOUNCE BACK

In basketball, if you miss the basket, the rebound gives you a second chance to score. Winning teams always use that second chance. They don't waste much time feeling mad or sorry for themselves. This is something they learned. Maybe you have a lot of natural bounce and you are good at trying again. But most of us have to train ourselves not to get discouraged or let certain things bother us so much. When things happen that get you down, bounce back up and say, "Things will get better," "I can still be okay," or "I can try again, or I'll try something else that works better."

 Don't waste time feeling sorry for yourself. Use your energy to try again or try another way. People who learn to bounce back get to do more things in life.

One way you bounce back is by getting perspective. You look at what happened from a few angles to see what it's all about. One of the first things we see by looking from a new perspective is that it's not all about us. Some things just happen. It's not our fault. It's not even personal. It just is.

Another way to bounce back is to get a new dream or project. You can find that dream or project by paying attention to your daydreams. Making sure you have enough time to relax helps you feel the feelings and also makes room for new ideas. If you give yourself healing time and daydreaming time, you'll start bouncing back sooner than you think.

Bouncing back also means you can make fun of things. So when things seem grim, try to lighten up and find something funny or even ridiculous in what's happening.

Justin always had lots of stuff going back and forth to his two homes. He started calling his landing and take-off pads JMX and JDX for Justin's Mom airport and Justin's Dad's airport.

How to Help Wishes and Dreams Come True

Feel How It Would Be If the Dream Came True

In Max's daydream, he has friends who are fun and loyal. He sees them all going on day trips and learning karate together. He feels liked and happy. He gets a smile on his face just thinking about it. He's not sure his mom would approve of the sport, so that's a consideration. (During this daydream, Max forgets about his disagreement with his stepmom that morning.)

Angela feels herself jumping and scoring at the volleyball net during an important game, then getting high fives from her teammates. She feels really great. (While Angela daydreams, she doesn't give her parents' divorce a thought.)

Doug feels excited as he imagines himself talking in Japanese with some of his classmates. Then he imagines the smells and sounds of going into the city's Japanese neighborhood shops and talking to the shopkeepers. (Doug has some sad thoughts about his mom's wedding day, but he shoos them away and gets back to his daydreaming.)

```
TIP
```
The feelings you have when you daydream are just as important as your dream. When feelings are positive, they give you the encouragement to work toward your goal.

```
TIP
```
Always, always, be the good guy in your daydream, and always dream what it would be like to succeed. That's one of the jobs of daydreaming. Keep on imagining. No fair bringing in negative ideas or sad thoughts like, "That could never happen" or "No one would ever approve of that." Negative thoughts take away a dream's power.

Follow Your Ideas and Questions When You Think about Your Dream

As you imagine and feel what it could be like to get your wish, something quietly wonderful can happen. You might start getting more ideas and details of what you would need to do and how that could feel. These details make your dream more and more real and make you more curious about the subject of your wish. Maybe you go to the library and take out a book or DVD. If your parents are on the Internet (and they give you permission), you can get information there. You can also learn more by hanging around someone who is actually doing it or knows about it.

Max doesn't make friends easily. But he is interested in karate, so he followed that idea first. He went to the library and got a book about it. When he was reading the book at school, another kid asked him about it. They liked each other and started eating lunch together.

Angela hung out more at volleyball practices and watched the strategies of the best players. She got up her courage to talk to one of them and asked what it takes to make the team. Now she has an idea of what she has to do.

Doug found a classmate who spoke Japanese and he learned how to say "good" and "good-bye." His classmate offered to teach him twenty words if Doug would help him with his math.

For all these kids, first there was a daydream. Then pieces of that dream started to be real. Those first small steps are how dreams start to come true.

Keep a "Considerations" List

Max's considerations list includes his mom's permission, transportation to the classes, paying for the classes, and not knowing exactly how to go about it. You can work with your list to make a wish or dream come true. It's made up of all those things that at first seem discouraging. Max sets a goal to talk to his mom about all the considerations on his list. Set one small goal for yourself and start doing things to reach it. Then set another small goal. Then another. Give yourself a high five or a thumbs-up when you reach each of these goals. Giving yourself credit for every goal you reach is another way you train your brain. Celebrate your accomplishments! Here is how it could work.

Max and his new friend talked about learning karate. Max set a small goal of finding at least two places that had classes. He looked in the phone book, made calls, and found them *(high five!)*. He set another small goal to visit these places with his dad and find out about classes. It took a few weeks, but he met that goal, too *(high five!)*. Max now feels that learning karate is possible. His friend might take the class, too. Max realizes that if he takes the class, he will meet other guys who could become friends. He's getting excited. His dream is getting real.

After talking with his mom, he got permission *(high five!)*. But she cannot provide transportation, and she can pay for only half the cost of classes *(groan)*. Max is disappointed. But now he has to bounce back. The process of reaching any goal always has temporary roadblocks like this. Max has to pick himself up and try again or try another way. He has to think about what the next step will be.

When you get information, set small goals, and start feeling enthusiastic, things can happen. Max is finding out how to take things one small step at a time. Keep piling up your small goals until you've reached your big goal (or something else just as good).

Max has two goals left—finding transportation and half the cost of the karate classes. He calls his dad and asks him for ideas on transportation and how to pay for half the class. His dad says he can pay for half the cost *(high five!)*, but he can't help with transportation. So Max has to bounce back again because he still needs transportation. Luckily, Max's friend also gets permission to take the class, and his friend's mom said she would drive. *(High fives all around! Max is now ready to learn karate, his original goal, and he has made one new friend already.)*

> **Small goals make dreams come true.**

Max feels good about himself and about his ability to get so close to what he wants. His good feelings are contagious. When a kid shows as much interest in something as Max has done, parents are impressed. Maybe once Max learns karate, he will love it. But what if he doesn't? He may still meet new kids there. And he can pick another sport or activity to do with friends. He now knows how to use his imagination and how to set small goals and follow through to get what he wants.

Usually, the bigger the dream, the longer the time it takes to reach it. You can get discouraged. So divide it up into smaller pieces, just like Max did. Sometimes you don't make your first big goal, especially if you lose interest or you believe deep down that it will never, ever happen no matter what. You also might change your goal halfway through because you want something different or better. Or parts of your dream can come true, even if all of it doesn't.

Just remember to bounce. If you don't make a goal, try it again. Maybe go about it a little differently, or make the goal a little different. Some people are lucky. They have a natural gift for making dreams come true, but most people have to take it step by step with small goals. And taking these small steps is something everyone can learn how to do.

 Daydreams or wishes can often encourage us to use our talents. Find out more about your strengths and

talents. Experts say there are at least eight different ways to be smart. Most everything we do uses at least two of these intelligences at once. Everyone has all eight, but most of us have two or three talents that are our strongest and easiest. Find out more about multiple intelligences in the "Extras" section.

GET MOVING WITH YOUR OWN DREAMS

Make some photocopies (at least five) of the worksheet on the next page. You need more than one copy because it's good to have more than one dream.

If you have a dream right now, you can begin filling out a worksheet. It can be a smaller dream, like going to a certain camp this summer. Or it can be a huge dream, like being an astronaut and traveling to Mars. Don't expect to be able to fill it all out at once. It takes time to think of ideas and goals—days, even weeks. You don't have to wait until the worksheet is complete to start taking the first small steps to make your dream come true.

It's okay if you don't have a dream in mind. Take your time and daydream. An idea will come to you. Deep down *everyone* has dreams.

If you need a parent's—or stepparent's—help to make your dream come true, you can share your worksheet with him or her to show that you are serious. Or you can keep your dream private if you are not ready to share it.

ONE OF MY DREAMS

My dream is _____

_____

If my dream was true, I would have these feelings

_____

Because _____

_____

I got these other ideas about my dream:

1. _____
2. _____
3. _____
4. _____

My considerations list:

1. _____ 4. _____
2. _____ 5. _____
3. _____ 6. _____

My first small goal is _____

My second small goal is _____

My third small goal is _____

You are on your way. Keep setting small goals till you reach your destination. If you don't reach all your small goals, try again later. Or change that small goal.

My reward for reaching my goal is _____

Make power daydreaming a habit. Feel how great it would be to have that daydream come true. Then, someday soon, pick up a copy of the worksheet "One of My Dreams" and start writing. You don't have to finish it. Just start. As Chapter 12 says, believe in yourself.

I will follow my dreams.

Chapter 11

What's True about Life

A s you travel down the road of your life, you will carry your own ideas and beliefs with you. What you believe about yourself is just as important as taking care of your body. Some beliefs and habits can help you focus, pick up your spirits, energize you to reach your goals, and help you have a lot of fun. Other beliefs and habits can bring you down, be hurtful, and make you feel like a failure or a victim. But you can make smart choices! You can believe in yourself.

YOU ARE AN ORIGINAL

There is no other person exactly like you on earth. You have something special to give to others and to yourself. That's a fact. That doesn't make you or me better than others, but it does make each of us an original.

Each of us has something special that no one else has or has ever had. Not before we were born and not even now. We have our own way to feel, to think, and to see and hear things. So believe in yourself and that you have something special. Being the best person you can be right now already makes you a star (even if people sometimes don't appreciate that fact). Try to remember this when things get goofy at home or there's trouble with friends or you're disappointed in yourself. Pick yourself up and tell yourself that, one step at a time, you can figure out what's best for you.

THINKING TRAPS ARE GROSS

Anyone can have a thinking trap. Have you ever thought, "I'm not good enough," "I don't fit in," "My life is hopeless," "I'm ugly," "I can't do anything right"? Has anyone ever said these things to you about you? Sometimes these repulsive thoughts can repeat in your head over and over like a TV commercial. These are the "repulsive repeats" and a very clever thinking trap. Ugh! Ick! Gross! Train your brain to get rid of them.

YOU CAN TRAIN YOUR BRAIN

TYB

You can talk to yourself silently in a nice way. Say to yourself, "I believe in myself. Those are just repulsive repeats. They are not true." Save your energy for positive thoughts. Poke fun at these negative or scary thoughts: "The repulsives are here. Bring out the bug spray." Or have a picture in your mind of hosing the bad feelings down a drain. Then do something you know will make you feel good, such as playing with your pet or picking something from your "feel good" list. Don't be rude. Talk nicely to yourself. Don't put yourself down. As Paul wrote, "Stay positive. Never think negative!" That's the big key.

YOU CAN MAKE SMART CHOICES

What's true about making choices is that the more information you have, the better choices you make. The problem solvers in this book are one way to think things through. Other ways are to think, look closely, listen to yourself. Watch what people you admire do. Will their actions really give them a good life? You can also talk to people you trust and get their ideas on the best choices. For example, your parents have told you that you can go out for a sport or take lessons or go to an after-school club, but that you can do only two of them, no more. But you want to do three things, not just two. Which two will you choose? Talk it over with friends, your parents, coaches, teachers, or club sponsors. Find out how much time these activities will actually take, how tough the practices and classes are, and what really happens there. Then choose for yourself.

YOU CAN REPAIR BAD CHOICES

There are poor choices and bad choices. Poor choices are everyday things we do that we wish later we hadn't done. We can repair them fairly easily. Everyone makes some poor choices sometimes. No one is perfect. Maybe you made a choice not to study for that math test and got a D. Maybe you didn't clean out that cut on your hand and it's now infected. Maybe you forgot your new shoes at the beach or yelled mean things to a sibling. You already know what to do to repair these poor choices.

Then there are big, bad choices. These are choices that mess up your life. They can put you in real danger or get you in serious trouble. Look at the list below. Are any of these things happening to you?

BAD CHOICES: IS THIS HAPPENING TO YOU? A LITTLE? A LOT? NO?

- Exploding with intense anger or having big upsets at home or at school

- Big-time mouthing off at parents, teachers, coaches

- Being really obnoxious or making big trouble

- Cheating and lying about schoolwork or activities

- Lying to parents about important and dangerous things

- Being a bully or being bullied

- Hurting yourself with an eating disorder like bulimia or anorexia, cutting yourself, or being excessively overweight

- Drinking, smoking pot, doing drugs

- Getting into sex and "hooking up"

You Don't Have to Be a Victim

If any of these things are happening a lot (or even a little), take a deep breath and tell yourself this: "I can change this for the better. I know I'm a kid, but I can help myself. I need time and the right kind of help. I am worth it. I can do it. I deserve a good life, and I deserve to be successful." Then tell your parent or an adult you trust about it *immediately*.

It is easy to have our brains and bodies kidnapped by certain bad feelings and situations. It is tough to pull out of these behaviors and dangers alone. Everyone needs a parent, a pal, or a coach to help find better ways to be well and safe. You deserve to be the best person you can be. Sure, it will take effort, but you can do it, no matter how hard it is or how long it takes. Find those people who care about you. Let them help. You deserve to treat yourself right.

YOU CAN TAKE CARE WITH YOUR FEELINGS

Your feelings are important. Feelings are a part of you. Taking care of your feelings means getting to know what you are feeling and what you do because of it. Going through changes like divorce or a new stepfamily usually means having lots of feelings and special energy. Remember the "feeling soup" on page 12? Most kids know when they are sad or mad, but not everyone knows how to explain the way they feel when they are discouraged, scared, or disrespected. Some kids have stomachaches or headaches that are caused by certain feelings. Some kids feel angry, others feel bad about themselves. Other kids react differently altogether.

Figure out how to pay attention to what you are feeling. Pick it out and get curious. When does this feeling usually pop up? Give it a name. Watch and listen to what other people call a feeling. Maybe you usually have a feeling when a certain kid looks at you in a snobby or stuck-up way. Would you say you feel embarrassed? Maybe you get mad, or maybe you feel you are really not as good as the stuck-up kid. You can't change how that kid acts, but you can get smart about what you are feeling and give it a name. It actually helps. When we know what we feel and how it affects us, it is easier to rebound from disappointment and stress. Try not to skip over this idea. It's not just a part of growing up and knowing yourself, it's also part of getting smarter about life and people.

Feelings are always real. But they are not always smart. Sometimes feeling mad or sad or panicky can be in charge of what you do or say. This could be trouble if you don't think about the consequences—that is, what will happen after you do or say something. When you don't think about the consequences, it means your feelings are in charge of what you do instead of your brain or what your heart knows is the right thing to do. *So, try to remember that even though feelings are always real, they are not always smart.*

What if you are mad at a kid for taking your favorite spot at lunch? You let your mad feelings take over and you shove him and say that he is stupid in front of other kids. Later you find out he is in charge of picking who's going to be on the school newspaper in your school—and you really want to write the sports column. The consequences of your pushy behavior might be that you look like a bully to others *and* you might not make it on the newspaper.

Body smarts. Some feelings we have in our body are not emotions at all but "sensations." These are another set of ancient bodily reactions that alert us to something important. For some reason, we also call them "feelings" just as we would if we were feeling sad. (It can be confusing, but that's the English language for you!) These sensations in our bodies can give us important signals about what's happening around us in our environment.

For example, you meet a new person and you have a restless or even a sinking or strange feeling around your belly. Later you might find out that the person does sneaky things and doesn't tell the truth. Your first feelings in your body were a signal for you to be careful. We call this a "gut feeling." You might get a prickly feeling or goose bumps. Sometimes that could mean you are cold and need to put on a sweater. But other times it can mean something really important is happening for you to pay attention to. Maybe someone is talking to you, or something you see scares you, or you are getting on the bus. So look around. If you are watching a scary movie, you know it's the movie. Otherwise, your body is telling you that something near you might be dangerous. These gut feelings aren't emotions, but they are your own "body smarts." Whatever you want to call them, *pay attention to them.*

YOU CAN HAVE SOMEONE TO LOOK UP TO

Do you have a role model? Someone you think is great? Maybe someone who is really good at something or has a job you would like to have someday? Some kids wish they could be like a parent or another relative. Others admire a celebrity, a star athlete, a teacher, an older kid, someone from history, or even a person in a book or movie.

If you can admire your parents, you are in luck! You get to watch closely how they do things. They can be your coaches. But remember, you are not exactly the same person as your mom or dad. Even if you look alike, you still are you and not an exact copy of them. This is good. You are meant to be the best you that you can be, not a copy of someone else. For example, Molly looks just like her dad, who is a great musician. She thinks she should also be a musician, but she secretly likes math and sports better. Sometimes kids or parents are disappointed if a child is not exactly like a parent, but it's not the kid's fault. Everyone is an original.

Remember Luke? He admires his uncle and is trying to be like him. He now thinks of his dad as almost two people. He appreciates and loves that part of his dad that was good with mechanics and sports and was sometimes sweet to him. But there is also a part of Dad that did bad things. Luke knows that even though he looks a lot like his father, he isn't his dad. He is Luke. He can admire and copy what he likes about his dad and not get trapped by the bad stuff.

You Can Protect Yourself from Certain Illnesses

People can learn to protect themselves from developing illnesses that run in families such as diabetes, heart trouble, or alcoholism. When an illness runs in a family, it means that family members could develop that illness easily. Luke, his uncle, and his mom are taking classes to learn about his dad's problem with drinking. Luke is learning what to do to protect himself from becoming an alcoholic.

You Can Have Fun and Enjoy Yourself

When families change, there's lots of stuff that's interesting along with the things you don't like. But, you are a kid! Kids are experts at finding ways to have fun, no matter what. Even though some adults might forget this about kids, *kids are meant to be curious, to be enthusiastic, to have fun.* This is one of the ways kids learn and grow. So find time to set aside any troubles you have and *just have fun with your friends and families.* The saying "Laughter is the best medicine" is also true about enjoying life.

> I'm a kid and I'm an expert at having fun!

Chapter 12

Believe in Yourself

Traveling the road of separation, divorce, and stepfamily life will give you many kinds of opportunities, even when the road is bumpy. Use this time to get new skills, to know yourself better, and bounce back and try again.

YOU CAN HAVE HEART

When someone tells you that you have heart, it means you have courage. You believe in yourself and in what you are doing and in your goals. You do your best. A person with heart stays with something even when things get tough. It's a deep believing that you can make it. It also means you have hope for your future. If someone says you have a big heart, it also means you are generous and caring and that you reach out to help others. When you have a big heart, everyone wants to be around you.

KNOW YOU CAN DO IT!

No matter what happens to you anytime in your life, things will always go better when you believe in yourself and have heart. This is true whether your parents are married, separated, divorced, living with someone, or remarried. It's true all your life, whether you are eight or eighty. Remember this when you feel sad, hyper, scared, depressed, or stressed, or even if you feel like you're at the bottom of a big pile of stuff. Look for what you can learn from the experience and don't get clobbered with thoughts that say nothing will ever turn out right for you. Things can get better. *Do not give up on yourself, ever. Have heart!*

A year or two from now, you could look back and see how far you have advanced. You could have already made a bunch of smaller dreams come true; be sharper about your feelings; friends, activities, and solving problems; and be much smarter about life. You could say, "I really did a lot! I can make decisions about what to do and what to be. I am important to myself and others. I make a difference."

You now know that no matter what happens in your family, you can go on to have a happy and successful life. So, if things look messed up at times, remember tomorrow is another day and you get another chance for something better. Do not give up on yourself, ever, ever, ever.

Have heart and have a great life!

> I believe in myself. I have heart.
>
> I will have a great life.

PART IV

EXTRAS

Books

Amber Brown Wants Extra Credit, by Paula Danziger

Basic Social Skills for Youth, by Boys Town

The Behavior Survival Guide for Kids: How to Make Good Choices and Stay Out of Trouble, by Tom McIntyre

Bringing Up Parents: The Teenager's Handbook, by Alex J. Packer

Dear Mr. Henshaw, by Beverly Cleary

Getting Even, by Mavis Jukes

Help! A Girl's Absolutely Indispensable Guide to Divorce and Stepfamilies, by Nancy Holyoke

Highs! Over 150 Ways to Feel Really REALLY Good Without Alcohol or Other Drugs, by Alex Packer

It's Not the End of the World, by Judy Blume

Make Believe, by Susan Beth Pfeffer

My Mother Got Married (And Other Disasters), by Barbara Park

No B. O.! by Marguerite Crump

The Reason for Janey, by Nancy Hope Wilson

The Right Moves to Getting Fit & Feeling Great! by Tina Schwager and Michele Schuerger

The 7 Habits of Highly Effective Teens, by Sean Covey

Stick Up for Yourself! Every Kid's Guide to Personal Power and Positive Self-Esteem, by Gershen Kaufman, Lev Raphael, and Pamela Espeland

The Suitcase Kid, by Jacqueline Wilson

Too Old for This, Too Young for That! by Harriet S. Mosatche and Karen Unger

You and the Rules in Your Family, by Lea MacAdam

You're Smarter Than You Think: A Kid's Guide to Multiple Intelligences, by Thomas Armstrong and Jennifer Brannen

What Do You Really Want? How to Select a Goal and Go for It! by Beverly K. Bachel

What in the World Do You Do When Your Parents Divorce? A Survival Guide for Kids, by Kent Winchester and Roberta Beyer

What Teens Need to Succeed, by Peter L. Benson, Judy Galbraith, and Pamela Espeland

Web Resources

www.kidsturn.org The Kids' Turn Web site is about separation and divorce, with sections for kids, parents, answers to questions, kids' artwork, calendars to print, and other activities.

www.Kidscape.org.uk This Web site is dedicated to preventing bullying and abuse of children, with sections for kids and sections for adults, and ways to help yourself.

www.KidsHealth.org This Web site has sections for kids, teens, and adults, with articles on recipes, first aid, feelings, how to beat stress, and more.

www.GirlScouts.org This is the official Web site of the Girl Scouts of the USA, with sections for girls and teens and activities, quizzes, video games, and other activities.

www.YMCA.net The Young Men's Christian Association (YWCA for women) site has information on Y activities such as swimming pool hours, exercise classes, and camping trips in your area.

www.Scouting.org Information about national activities for kids who are in scouting and on how to start a troop in your area.

www.girlsandboystown.org Boys Town, started in 1919 to provide home and community for kids, tells its history, describes its other sites and programs, and gives stories of happy alumni.

www.bgca.org The Boys and Girls Clubs of America have programs in leadership, technology, art, recreation, etc., in its 3,000 clubhouses, and its Web site has lots of games and TV shows.

www.usdoj.gov/domesticviolence.htm This Web site is sponsored by the U.S. Department of Justice. The National Domestic Violence Hotline (1-800-799-7233) answers twenty-four hours a day so you can get information about help near you. Or call 911.

Sample Problem Solvers and Worksheets

TIP *You might want to use a workbook or folder to keep your worksheets or the ideas you picked up from reading or naming your feelings. You might keep these ideas in your journal, or you might want them separate.*

SIX-STEP SOLUTION
DAVID'S TOO-LONG COMMUTE

David's father changed jobs and had to move farther away from school. David had a choice either to change schools in the middle of the year or to get up forty-five minutes earlier to make it to his old school. He chose to get up earlier. He felt tired most of the time and his schoolwork wasn't as good as before, but he didn't want to change schools yet. So David did a smart thing. He tried the problem solver before he talked to his mom or dad.

1. **Nail it with words—three ways.**
   What David wrote:

   a. What is my situation? When I stay with Dad on school nights, the commute to school is too long.

b. **What is my goal?** I would like the commute to be shorter or not be at Dad's so much on school days.

c. **What's standing in my way?** Mom works nights now and Dad lives where he lives, so I feel bad about even bringing it up.

2. **Think about what could happen.**

a. **What could happen if I reach my goal?** I think I wouldn't feel so tired and my schoolwork would pick up.

b. **What could happen if I don't reach my goal?** I worry that I'll feel more tired and fail some classes.

3. **Search for ideas to get around what's standing in your way.**

I could talk to Dad and Mom about this and ask them to come up with a solution.

I could ask other kids what they do when the commute is long.

I could ask my grandmother to talk to Dad and Mom about this for me.

4. **Look at each idea closely.** For each idea, ask yourself, "If I choose this idea, then what might happen?"

If I talk to Dad, he's going to want good ideas for solving this. Mom already feels bad because she has to work nights and I have to commute, so I don't want to make her feel worse.

If I asked other kids what they do, it might help, but my situation is really different from theirs.

Maybe my grandmother will have an idea. My grandmother might help me with the words to use to talk to my dad and mom.

5. **Choose one or two of the best ideas.** ✓ ✓ Then start working on one or both of them.

David decided to talk with his grandmother. Because David had gone through the solution steps, he was able to express himself more clearly when he talked to her. His grandmother listened carefully and then suggested that he stay with her two school nights the rest of the school year. She lived close to the school. She and David talked with his mom and dad, and everyone decided it was a good solution.

6. **Review.** ⟮ ☺ ⟯ After you've given your idea a chance to work, ask yourself, "What's working well? Should changes be made?"

Six weeks later, Grandmother, David, Mom, and Dad were satisfied that the arrangement is working well enough for everyone. But his mom wondered if living in three places a week was making his life more complicated. David says he feels better and his grades are improving. David also says that when this semester is over, he will either switch schools or his mom will be able to work days again and he can stay with her and in the same school.

Copy this page so you can try this yourself.

SIX-STEP SOLUTION

1. **Nail it with words—three ways.**
   (Write your answers below.)

   a. What's my situation?

   _____

   b. What's my goal?

   _____

   c. What's standing in my way?

   _____

2. **Think about what could happen?**

   a. What could happen if I reach my goal?

   _____

   b. What could happen if I don't reach my goal?

   _____

3. **Search for ideas to get around what's standing in your way.** *(Write each idea on the idea line below, don't but answer "Then what?" yet.)*

Idea:_____

Then what?_____

Idea:_____

Then what?_____

Idea:_____

Then what?_____

4. **Look at each idea closely.** For each idea, ask yourself, "If I choose this idea, then what might happen?" (*Now* write your "Then what?" answers above.)

5. **Choose one or two of the best ideas.** Then start working on one or both of them.

   Idea 1 _____

   Idea 2 _____

6. **Review.** After you've given your idea a chance to work, ask yourself, "What's working well? What changes should be made?"

   (If you need to make changes, be sure to ask what might happen if you make that change, just like you did in step 3. Then do steps 4, 5, and 6 again.)

Congratulations! Now, reward yourself!

GINA'S MUSIC CAMP
SOLVING THE PUZZLE

Gina plays the flute. She wants to go to a music camp this summer. She thinks it is expensive, and she doesn't know how to ask her parents about it. It's a puzzle. How can she explain it to her parents so she has the best chance of getting what she wants? She has to find two prize pieces to her puzzle. The first piece is her attitude and the words she uses when she talks to her parents about her wish. This piece is made up of her most positive statements. She can't blame or be mad or be rude. The second piece is finding alternatives. That means she has to find out what else she could do that would either be just as good as going to music camp or still be something that involved music over the summer. This is how this problem solver works.

Finding Gina's Prize Puzzle Pieces

---

1. Write your goal or situation.

Gina wrote: I want to go to music camp. It's expensive and my parents will probably say they can't afford it.

---

2. Write your feelings about it.

Gina wrote: I really want to go! I've worked hard all year. I always practice my flute. I deserve to go. **I hate** *feeling like we are* **so poor** *now that there are* **no** *extras.*

The **bold words** are negative. Look at what Gina wrote. See how the negative words could make her parents stop listening?

3. Prize Piece 1

Rewrite it. Make it positive!

Gina rewrote her feelings: I love my music. I have practiced hard all year. I want to keep it up this summer, like at this music camp. I know my parents are doing the best they can. This camp would be great if they can do it. My friend is going, too.

This says what she wants to say, but it's much easier to listen to and it sounds fair.

Check your attitude.

4. Prize Piece 2

Find one or two other alternatives.

Gina wrote: I could ask for extra lessons. There is also a music class at the Y this summer. Maybe I could do some jobs for Mom or Dad, or earn some of the money another way.

Some kids feel that to think of alternatives is like "giving in." It's not. It shows adults you are thoughtful, sincere about your goal, and not selfish.

Now that Gina has her two prize pieces from Boxes 3 and 4, she is ready to talk to her parents. She will use her positive words from Box 3 first. Her parents can listen to her without feeling pressured by her negative feelings. Maybe they say yes, she can go to music camp. That's perfect. But what if they say, "Not this year" or "You can go for one week, but not two"? Whatever they say, Gina also has her ideas from Box 4 to talk about (summer school class, extra lessons, a job). They will be interested to hear that she wants to keep up her music over the summer no matter what.

Finding the two prize pieces in any situation is an important life skill for many things. Get into the habit of expressing yourself in a positive way and having other alternatives. It really works.

THE PRIZE PUZZLE PIECES

Copy this page so you can try this yourself.

1. Write your goal or situation.

_____

_____

_____

_____

2. Write your feelings about it.

_____

_____

_____

_____

When you are finished writing, go back
and circle any negative words.

3. Prize Piece 1
Rewrite it. Make it positive!

_____

_____

_____

_____

Check your attitude.

4. Prize Piece 2
Find one or two other alternatives.

_____

_____

_____

_____

Now you are ready to make your request
or discuss it with others.

Thank You

M any kids, young adults, parents, counselors, therapists, mediators, teachers, and lawyers have contributed to this book. I am deeply grateful for their ideas, for their encouragement, and especially for their generosity of spirit and commitment to children. I asked them many questions, and their answers were wise and practical.

Thank you to all those who reviewed the manuscript at different stages—sometimes twice or three times: Jennifer Frazer; Jane Merryman; Kacey Wanland; Rudi A. J. M. Yniguez; Tracey Weddle; Rita Frischer; Janet Zarem; Jennifer Middleton; Amy Firstman; Zoe Szekley; Jennifer Rockwell; Lonner Holden; Olivia Holden; Susan M. Johnson; Penny Warner, MA; Andrew Firstman, MS; AJ Firstman; Emily Brown, LCSW; Gail Fisher, JD, MSS, MLSP; Nancy Oelson, PhD; Angelique Basu, MD.

A special thank-you to the *Kids Turn* organization of the San Francisco Bay Area and its executive director Claire Barnes, MA, and program director Elyse Jacobs, MFA, for including me in their work with the *Kids Turn* workshops and symposiums. A big thank-you to the workshop coordinators—Diana Blank, LCSW; Christina LaGrave, MA; Danielle Richardson, PhD—and to the workshop leaders I worked with, especially Silvia MacAllister, LMFT; Selena Lowe Hong, MS; Lynette

Jones, BA; Dena Selix, MEd; and Dorie Rosenberg, MEd, MS. Thanks also to Cathy Hanville, LCSW. Thank you to Beverly Upton, executive director of the San Francisco Domestic Violence Consortium and Partners Ending Domestic Abuse for her careful reviews and suggestions for the "Protect Yourself" chapter and the folks at the National Domestic Violence Hotline for their help.

To my treasured friends and colleagues Phil Reedy, MA, and Linda Delbar, RN, at *The New Family Center,* and to my agent George Nicholson, you inspired me with your steadfast dedication to children, your support of my vision, and your belief in this book. Thank you for your humor, for sharing your many years of experience, for your ongoing support, and for your many patient reviews and expert suggestions. Special thanks to Kathleen Erickson of Erickson Editorial, a dear friend and local editor, for her insights, support, expert consultation, and guidance throughout the many days of writing and rewriting. My heartfelt thanks to my editor Nancy Hancock at Fireside and to Sarah Peach and the rest of the Fireside team. You all embraced this new type of book from its beginnings, asked the tough questions, valued the vision, and saw the book through its final design and publication. I am very grateful.

Finally, I want to thank all the kids and parents I've worked and talked with over the years for sharing their lives, their successes, their challenges, and their wisdom. You continue to inspire me.

Index

About the Author

Isolina Ricci, Ph.D., author of the enduring classic for parents, *Mom's House, Dad's House* is an internationally renowned consultant, lecturer, and educator whose work has inspired two generations of divorcing and remarried parents with her message that they can bring strength and dignity to their families, regardless of their marital status or custody arrangement.

Many of her pioneering concepts such as "Parenting Plans," two homes for children, meeting children's needs, and ways for parents to work together have become accepted standards and her work has been cited in courtrooms and numerous publications. In addition to her clinical and educational work, she has conducted research at Stanford University on divorce and child adjustment and headed the Statewide Office of Family Court Services for the California Judicial branch for fifteen years, providing professional training and consultation to all California family courts. She is the recipient of the Distinguished Mediator Award from the Academy of Family Mediators and is a Rockefeller Bellagio scholar.

Dr. Ricci is the director of the New Family Center and divides her time between consulting with family courts, working with families, and *Kids Turn,* a nonprofit organization dedicated to giving children a voice when their parents divorce or remarry. Visit her at www.isolinaricci.com.

3 1221 08268 0112

The time-tested guide for parents and professionals.

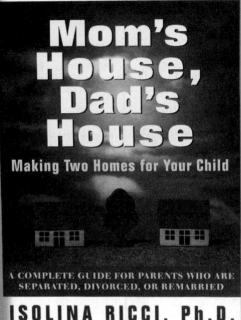

THE GROUNDBREAKING CLASSIC
COMPLETELY REVISED AND UPDATED

Mom's House, Dad's House

Making Two Homes for Your Child

A COMPLETE GUIDE FOR PARENTS WHO ARE
SEPARATED, DIVORCED, OR REMARRIED

ISOLINA RICCI, Ph.D.

0-684-83078-7

"The definitive hands-on resource."
—*Juvenile and Family Court Journal*

"The new edition is even better than the first, if that is possible…it is must reading for any parent transiting divorce and any professional who seeks to help them."
—*Family and Conciliation Courts Review*

Available wherever books are sold or at www.simonsays.com

FIRESIDE
A Division of Simon & Schuster